FIRST GENERATION

36 TRAILBLAZING IMMIGRANTS AND REFUGEES WHO MAKE AMERICA GREAT

BY SANDRA NEIL WALLACE AND RICH WALLACE   ILLUSTRATED BY AGATA NOWICKA

LITTLE, BROWN AND COMPANY
NEW YORK BOSTON

Little, Brown and Company
Hachette Book Group
1290 Avenue of the Americas, New York, NY 10104
Visit us at LBYR.com

First Edition: September 2018

Little, Brown and Company is a division of Hachette Book Group, Inc. The Little, Brown name and logo are trademarks of
Hachette Book Group, Inc.

The publisher is not responsible for websites (or their content) that are not owned by the publisher.

Library of Congress Cataloging-in-Publication Data
Names: Wallace, Sandra Neil, author. | Wallace, Rich, author. | Nowicka, Agata, illustrator.
Title: First generation: 36 trailblazing immigrants and refugees who make America great / by Sandra Neil Wallace & Rich
Wallace; illustrated by Agata Nowicka.
Other titles: Thirty six trailblazing immigrants and refugees who make America great | 36 trailblazing immigrants and refugees
who make America great
Description: First edition. | New York: Little, Brown and Company, [2018] | Includes bibliographical references. |
Audience: Ages 8–12.
Identifiers: LCCN 2017047847 | ISBN 9780316515245 (hardcover) | ISBN 9780316515238 (ebook)
Subjects: LCSH: Immigrants—United States—Biography—Juvenile literature. | Refugees—United States—Juvenile literature.
Classification: LCC E184.A1 W2165 2018 | DDC 305.9/06912—dc23
LC record available at https://lccn.loc.gov/2017047847

ISBNs: 978-0-316-51524-5 (hardcover), 978-0-316-52369-1 (ebook), 978-0-316-51523-8 (ebook), 978-0-316-52371-4 (ebook)

Printed in China

APS

10 9 8 7 6 5 4 3 2

The illustrations for this book were done digitally. This book was edited by Deirdre Jones and designed by Karina Granda. The
production was supervised by Virginia Lawther, and the production editor was Marisa Finkelstein. The text was set in Bembo
Book MT Std, and the display type is Harman Deco.

For Anna Koenig,
a first-generation trailblazer
who inspires us every day
—SNW and RW

For my daughter, Mila
—AN

★ CONTENTS ★

FIRST GENERATION

first gen·er·a·tion

1. The first members of a family to immigrate to a new country*

2. Children who are born in that new country to immigrant parents

*The people featured in this book all fit the first definition.

INTRODUCING THE HEROES OF
FIRST GENERATION

The United States is a nation of diversity, from Native American peoples to immigrants and refugees. Maybe you can trace your family back to the first colonists who came over from Europe, or to immigrants who arrived during the late 1800s. But immigrants and refugees didn't just come to this country hundreds of years ago. There are millions of new Americans making this country thrive right now.

You search the Internet thanks to an American inventor from Moscow, drink soda from an American mega-company led by a woman born in India, and listen to rock 'n' roll music performed by a guitarist who grew up in Mexico. If you've ever hiked in a national park, it's because of a Scottish-born naturalist with a passion to save the outdoors. So why don't people know about these inspirational new Americans? Whatever the reason, we felt it was time you did.

The thirty-six immigrants and refugees featured in this book have shaped our country in countless ways, from the development of electricity to the yogurt you might have eaten for breakfast. They represent many races, ethnicities, and religions. They are men and women from tiny villages in Africa and crowded cities in Europe and Asia. They were born in countries ranging from Somalia to Germany, Syria to China. They are artists, chefs, activists, athletes, and scientists. Most of them faced discrimination while they created meaningful, impactful lives in the United States. But they never gave up, because they believed in themselves and in the best of America.

These first-generation heroes were brave, whether coming to a new country by choice or fleeing here to save their lives. They embody American ideals by working hard, creating change, influencing others, and helping to guide the world. Albert Einstein and Maryam Mirzakhani, for instance, changed how people view science and mathematics. Dikembe Mutombo showed that athletes can lead in areas well beyond a playing field or court. Rose Winslow and Razia Jan saw wrongs and made them right, inspiring others to follow.

Whether you're first generation, tenth generation, or indigenous to this country, we hope the heroes in this book inspire you to blaze a trail yourself, and that they remind all Americans that our country's greatest strengths are its inclusiveness and diversity.

—Sandra Neil Wallace and Rich Wallace

HALIMA ADEN

"YOU DON'T HAVE TO CHANGE YOURSELF OR YOUR BELIEFS TO BE SUCCESSFUL."

Halima Aden was born in Kakuma Refugee Camp in northwestern Kenya in 1997 after her parents fled war-torn Somalia. Today, the overcrowded camp houses more than 180,000 refugees living in tin-roofed huts. Halima grew up there with kids from Sudan, Ethiopia, and Somalia. "It wasn't a matter of, 'Oh, we're in a refugee camp, my life sucks,'" she said. "It was 'Okay. We're in this predicament,' but you know, 'How do we go from here? What do we do?'" Halima and the other kids played together and learned Swahili to communicate. "As children, we were oblivious to race and religion," Halima recalled. When her family resettled in the United States, six-year-old Halima was surprised to see kids playing in separate groups instead of all together in her new city of St. Cloud, Minnesota.

As a Muslim, Halima chose to express her faith by wearing a hijab (headscarf) to cover her hair. At first, this was because she wanted to be just like her mother. "Every little girl looks up to her mom so much—that's your first hero," Halima explained. But she also felt best when she was dressed modestly. "It's how I interpret my religion," she said, even though some kids at school stared and bullied Halima and her hijabi friends. "It was a tough time—everyone wanted to be mean."

Flipping through magazines in her family home, Halima didn't find anyone who looked like her. So, after graduating from high school, she decided to enter the Miss Minnesota USA pageant. "Not seeing women that look like you in media in general and especially in beauty competitions sends the message that you're not beautiful or you have to change the way you look to be considered beautiful," Halima stressed. "And that's not true."

Halima was the first contestant to wear a hijab. She didn't win, but some of the world's top designers invited her to walk their runways during fashion weeks in New York City and Milan. She wore beautiful headscarves and flowing, loose-fitting dresses and pants. "When I'm walking the runway I want people to see that, yes, I'm wearing a hijab—but I'm also a million other things. I want us to get to a place where we just see women."

Halima Aden hadn't planned to be the first hijab-wearing model on the cover of an American beauty magazine. But that's what happened in 2017, and all because the Somali American woman refused to be anything but herself. "I think it's important to be diverse and I hope we continue to see that as a trend in the fashion industry."

★ Halima is the first hijabi to sign a contract with the world's biggest modeling agency.

★ Cinnamon-colored hijabs are Halima's favorite.

MADELEINE ALBRIGHT

"ONLY IN AMERICA CAN A REFUGEE BECOME THE SECRETARY OF STATE."

Madeleine Korbel Albright spent her childhood being brave. At the start of World War II in 1939, Nazis invaded her home country of Czechoslovakia (now the Czech Republic), and Madeleine and her family had to leave—*fast*. Her father worked as a diplomat representing their country around the world, so his life was in danger. They escaped to England, where Madeleine dodged bombs that destroyed buildings so close to her bedroom she could hear windows shattering. But she also saw people helping one another and sharing what little food they had. Those experiences stayed with Madeleine when she and her family came to the United States as refugees.

As a teenager in Denver, Madeleine didn't like being new in school or feeling different because of her accent. "I always felt I was a foreigner," she said. Her parents didn't have money for a car or a TV, so they invited people over to talk about the world's problems. Since Madeleine spoke four languages and loved learning about politics, the visitors valued her opinions. She began to see her background as her greatest strength.

Madeleine earned a scholarship to Wellesley College and studied political science. It was the first time she felt like she belonged, since everyone in her class was passionate about politics. She learned why countries went to war and how they made peace. "Being raised in a free America made all the difference," Madeleine said. That freedom made her question why more women weren't world leaders. She knew that societies thrive when women and men have equal opportunities.

Politicians were so impressed by Madeleine's views that she started working for the US government. As an ambassador to the United Nations, Madeleine worked to end the war and build peace in the Balkans, a region near her birth country. In 1996, President Bill Clinton chose Madeleine to be the US secretary of state, the most important international job in the country. Everyone in Congress agreed. It was the first time in American history that a woman held this office.

Madeleine loved the job, but she didn't like that critics talked about her clothes. They never did that with male diplomats. She made a statement by wearing a pin shaped from broken glass. It reminded people how she had broken through the glass ceiling of politics—a symbolic obstacle that kept women from being world leaders.

By breaking down barriers and embracing her heritage, Madeleine was able to create change in conflict countries. She saw beyond borders to the humanity in everyone, a quality that she says is very American. "We are a country," she explained, "that has been created and populated by people from other countries."

> * While she was in office, Madeleine found out that she is Jewish and that some of her relatives had been killed in concentration camps during World War II. Today, she is as proud of her Jewish heritage as she is of being America's first female secretary of state.
>
> * During World War II, Madeleine's parents secured fake passports to travel to England.

DIANA AL-HADID

"THE PROCESS OF MAKING SOMETHING IS A PROCESS OF LEARNING. IT'S MY LINK TO THE REST OF THE WORLD."

Diana Al-Hadid works *big*. Some of her sculptures fill entire rooms. Her studio includes a welding station, huge power drills, and assorted hammers and saws. Sometimes she wears a protective hazmat suit when she's carving. Working with heavy-duty materials such as steel, wood, fiberglass, and plaster, Diana creates sculptures that look like ruined cities, crumbling towers, and mythological worlds. "I climb over my sculptures. . . . They're very physical," she said, describing how she works. "I'll break things and then fix things, and sometimes I'm . . . literally inside the piece."

Diana's family left Aleppo, Syria, in 1986, when she was five years old. She spoke only Arabic when the Al-Hadids arrived in Ohio, and she quickly had to learn English. "I remember rehearsing saying 'I'm not from here, I'm from Syria,' but people didn't realize where Syria was." Though she fit in pretty well in her new neighborhood, Diana said her parents maintained strict traditions at home. "I wasn't allowed to go to prom," she said. "I wasn't allowed to have a boyfriend!" But she was free to pursue her love of art, and by the time she turned eleven, she was determined to be an artist.

Diana admired the Old Masters of Europe—painters like Goya, Botticelli, and Rembrandt—and she studied drawing and photography before turning to sculpture.

Sometimes her work draws on her Arab and Islamic background, but some critics have said she should do more to embrace those roots. "I am a Syrian artist, but that's not the full story," Diana said in reply. She is very concerned about the conflicts in war-torn Syria, where cities have been destroyed and thousands of people have been killed or have escaped as refugees. She also knows that opportunities for women in the arts and other professions were very limited in Syria even before the war. Living in the United States gave her the opportunity to create.

"Everything I do now is a product of my ancestry," Diana said. "I think that's a political enough statement: that I'm an Arab woman making sculptures. I wouldn't be making sculptures if I was living in Syria."

★ Diana's studio in Brooklyn, New York, used to be a silk flower factory.

★ Diana once put paint on the soles of her feet and danced to make a blueprint for a sculpture with her footsteps.

SERGEY BRIN

"THE U.S. HAD THE COURAGE TO TAKE ME AND MY FAMILY IN AS REFUGEES."

It started in a college dorm room and developed into one of the world's most powerful businesses. But long before Google founder Sergey Brin launched his company, he had a lot to overcome.

"I never felt like a part of the majority," Sergey said. He'd been a child in the Soviet Union, where Jewish people were banned from many things. His father had wanted to be an astronomer but wasn't allowed to attend graduate school because of his religion. He sneaked into classes and wrote a doctoral thesis anyway, and was eventually offered a teaching job at the University of Maryland, where he fled with his family in 1979.

In Maryland, six-year-old Sergey was teased by his classmates because of his heavy accent. But he was already used to being an outsider, and the private school he attended allowed him to explore his own interests. Working with puzzles, maps, and math games sparked his creativity. "I could grow at my own pace," he said.

Years later, Sergey attended Stanford University on a National Science Foundation scholarship and met a student named Larry Page. They argued a lot but could also see each other's intelligence, so they decided to work together, coming up with ways to link Internet pages. It was a risky venture, but after Sergey and Larry left Stanford they managed to scrape together enough money for equipment, and they continued to develop their project—which eventually grew into Google. (The name comes from the mathematical term *googol*—a one followed by one hundred zeroes.)

Sergey strongly believes in spreading knowledge, and Google helps people search the Internet by ranking how web pages are used. Its formula finds the most suitable sites based on how often they've been visited and on the significance of their links to other sites. The Google company reorganized to become Alphabet in 2015, with Sergey as president. Alphabet employs more than seventy thousand people and includes Google Maps, Gmail, the Android operating system, YouTube, and other highly successful offshoots.

In 2017, Sergey joined a protest against President Donald Trump's executive order that banned Syrian refugees and immigrants from entering the United States, as well as immigrants from Iran, Iraq, Libya, Somalia, Sudan, and Yemen—countries where the majority of the people are Muslims. Sergey knew from his family's experience in the Soviet Union that religious discrimination is wrong, and that opportunities in the United States had allowed immigrants like him to thrive. "I wouldn't be where I am today. . ." he said, "if this was not a brave country that really stood out and spoke for liberty."

★ The project that became Google was first called BackRub, because it relied on "back links" that pointed from one website to another.

★ Sergey exercises intensely and has competed in the diving World Masters Championships.

MARIA CONTRERAS-SWEET

"WE ARE ALL HERE TO BENEFIT AMERICA AND THIS IS THE FACE OF AN IMMIGRANT."

When Maria Contreras-Sweet was five years old, her family moved from Guadalajara, Mexico, to Los Angeles, California. She didn't speak English, and her kindergarten teacher disciplined her by tugging at her ears, thinking Maria wasn't paying attention. But the Contreras family did their best to adapt to their new life. Maria's single mother worked long hours at a meat-packaging plant so she could buy groceries for her six children. Maria recycled bottles and babysat. Then she took a job making bows in a flower shop.

"Whatever it was that I could do to bring money into the family, that's just what we did," Maria explained. "And I just remember one evening saying to [my mother], 'I don't know why we left our old country. What is in store for us?'" Her mother kept telling her that it was all worth it, because Maria would be working in an office someday. And after graduating from California State University, Maria surpassed her mother's expectations. By the time she turned twenty-four in 1979, Maria was the district manager of the US Census Bureau, overseeing eight hundred employees who documented California's population.

Maria soon realized that she was one of the few Latinas to reach this level in her career. "I looked to see who the successful businesses were run by; they weren't people who looked like me. And so I felt that we did need role models," she remembered. She became one herself as the first Latina cabinet secretary in California history. As the state's secretary of business, transportation, and housing, she built highways and buildings, and saw firsthand how the beautiful structures she helped create improved the lives of Californians and made the more than forty thousand employees she worked with proud.

Maria didn't stop there. She noticed how many times she'd seen minority families being denied loans to start their own businesses. So in 2006, she started ProAmérica Bank, a bilingual bank for California's Latinx small-business community. It's the accomplishment Maria's mother is most proud of. "A Latina had never started a bank," Maria explained. "The idea seemed impossible." But for one of the most successful Latinas in American business, it wasn't. Because of her drive and her determination to create opportunities for others to succeed, Maria has become a role model for young Americans.

* Maria served as the head of the US Small Business Administration under President Barack Obama.

* Maria never forgot about her childhood job. As an adult, she helped start California's bottle-recycling program.

CELIA CRUZ

"SINGING IS MY LIFE."

Úrsula Hilaria Celia de la Caridad Cruz Alfonso grew up in Havana, Cuba, in an extended family of fourteen people. Celia's father didn't earn much money working on the railroad, but he wanted the best life for his daughter and hoped she'd become a teacher. Celia instead took her grandmother's advice to heart: *Sing before starting a conversation.* And from the moment she started singing, Celia Cruz commanded attention.

She took bumpy bus rides around Cuba in the 1930s to perform in competitions. She won a cake in her first contest, singing a tango to the tapping of wooden sticks. Soon, Cubans waited by the radio to hear Celia and fell in love with her bold voice. Her big break came when the lead singer left the famous Cuban band La Sonora Matancera, and Celia was asked to fill in. "When opportunity presents itself, grab it," Celia said. She stayed with the group for fifteen years as the only woman in the band. She was also invited to perform at Havana's famous Tropicana club, where she developed a sense of style as explosive as her music. Squeezing into sequined gowns, wigs with bright feathers, and shiny shoes, Celia captured the spotlight.

But when Cuba's government changed to communism in 1959, Celia's performances in her home country ended. While she was touring Mexico, Cuban President Fidel Castro forbade Celia from returning home. Heartbroken that she couldn't even come back to see her dying mother, Celia immigrated to the United States and became an American citizen.

Celia's soulful Cuban sounds were an instant hit with Cuban Americans, who crowned her the Queen of Latin Music. But when salsa music was born in the streets of New York City, Celia switched over to these new Latin fusion sounds and made them famous. She knew her soulful singing was unique and lifted people's spirits. She started each show by shouting "*¡Azúcar!*" ("sugar"), energizing her audience like sugar energizes a body. "When people hear me sing I want them to be happy, happy, happy," Celia said. "My message is always *felicidad*—happiness."

Though salsa was dominated by male singers and musicians, Celia sold millions of records and became known as the Queen of Salsa. Late in her career, Celia reinvented herself by melding rap and hip-hop with her signature salsa sounds. By believing in her voice, Celia Cruz brought the world a bold new rhythm and thrilled millions of music fans with the sound of "*¡Azúcar!*"

* Celia won eight Grammy Awards and earned twenty-three gold records (meaning that a song or album sold at least half a million copies).

* Though fluent in English, Celia always sang in Spanish to honor the language of Cuban music and the roots of salsa.

* A school of music in the Bronx, New York, is named for Celia Cruz.

WILLEM DE KOONING

"I DON'T PAINT FOR A LIVING.
I PAINT TO LIVE."

Willem de Kooning didn't set out to be one of the world's most influential artists. He just wanted to paint, and spent his life learning how he could express the world through art.

Growing up in Rotterdam, the Netherlands, in the early 1900s, Willem always knew that he was an artist. So he quit school at age twelve and started working for a design firm. At night, he learned to draw at the famous Rotterdam Academy of Fine Arts and Techniques. But he had dreams of moving to America, hoping he'd earn more money and make his mark as a painter. He hid inside the engine room of a ship sailing for Virginia and landed there as a stowaway.

With no documents and knowing only one word of English (the word was *yes*), the twenty-two-year-old made his way to New York City. He painted houses during the week and created art on weekends. During the Great Depression of the 1930s, Willem painted wall murals inside government buildings. But he was forced to quit because he wasn't an American citizen.

Instead of getting discouraged, Willem spent his money on a radio to listen to while he painted. He discovered New York's thriving art community and became friends with artists like Jackson Pollock. Though he often felt insecure, he didn't believe in sticking to one style or movement. He painted solid brush strokes, blurry lines, people, and landscapes. Since no one else had painted that way before, the art world proclaimed that Willem and his friends had created a new movement called Abstract Expressionism.

But when Willem painted women, critics complained that they looked too fierce and that he'd abandoned abstract art. They said he was finished as an artist.

Willem didn't listen to the critics. He painted what he wanted and how he wanted. Now an American citizen, by 1962 Willem had become famous and earned a lot of money from his art, though he was never too old or too famous to stop learning. "You have to change to stay the same," Willem said. He studied in Japan and Italy. He created clay sculptures and paper drawings.

Sadly, dementia forced him to stop painting in 1991 at the age of eighty-seven. But Willem de Kooning's influence continues to inspire budding artists. By taking risks and refusing to stick to a single style, he became one of the most profound and influential painters in modern American history.

* The art school that Willem attended in Rotterdam is now called the Willem de Kooning Academie.

* If Willem didn't like one of his paintings, he'd throw it away.

* Willem's 1950 oil painting *Excavation* is considered a modern masterpiece.

VINOD DHAM

"I HAVE CONTINUOUSLY TAKEN RISKS IN MY CAREER AND IN THE PROCESS REINVENTED MYSELF MANY TIMES."

Vinod Dham is known as the Father of the Pentium Chip, a revolutionary invention that made computers, gaming systems, and other technology faster, more efficient, and less expensive. But when Vinod first arrived in the United States from India in 1975, he had only eight dollars in his pocket. Vinod's graduate studies at the University of Cincinnati included a job as a researcher, but he wouldn't be paid until he'd worked for a month! Fortunately, an employee of the university loaned Vinod $125 from a fund for foreign students. "She saved my butt," he said.

Vinod repaid the loan as soon as he started getting paychecks. But he struggled to adjust to American life. "It is very hard to come from a different culture into a new culture," he said. The university's professors tried to put him at ease, though, including one who gave Vinod his only B grade. The professor gave him another test, and the result was still a B, "but I thought that was so fair to even entertain the possibility of giving me a chance like that."

Vinod was hired as an engineer at a company called Intel, where he developed the Pentium chip that transformed the computer industry. He is quick to say that he didn't invent the chip, but that he took "what already was" and moved it "a step beyond." Vinod eventually reached the management level at Intel, demonstrating that he was more than a technology expert; he was great at running a company. He oversaw the multibillion-dollar business, focusing on the idea that technology can succeed only if it's affordable to the public.

After sixteen years at Intel, Vinod was ready for new challenges. "One of the best decisions I ever made was joining Intel," he said. "And the next-best decision was to leave." Since then, he's worked at "startup" companies like NexGen and Silicon Spice. Startups are new companies that often fail because they run out of money, so they usually rely on outside people to invest money in the company in exchange for owning part of it.

Vinod described the excitement and difficulties of working in a startup company this way: "You build something when everything is stacked up against you." His risk-taking attitude has remained the same throughout his career, and he believes that people should keep taking chances until they find the right method. "If the original idea fails, then pivot and persist."

* Vinod's charitable work includes support for HIV/AIDS prevention and for disadvantaged and orphaned children.

* President Bill Clinton appointed Vinod to his Advisory Commission on Asian Americans and Pacific Islanders.

CHERYL DIAZ MEYER

"JOURNALISM IS A CALLING, AND IF YOU TRULY FEEL THE CALL, FOLLOW YOUR HEART."

Gunfire blasted from both sides of the battle lines near Baghdad, Iraq. An injured civilian was trapped inside a burning van. As US Marines risked their lives to help, Cheryl Diaz Meyer conquered her fears and burst into action, too. "I was there to cover a war," Cheryl recalled. "I mentally prodded myself [to act]." Cheryl's photograph of two Marines dragging the injured man toward safety was broadcast to the world. Later, it earned Cheryl and her colleague David Leeson the 2004 Pulitzer Prize for Breaking News Photography.

As an embedded journalist, Cheryl was well aware of the risks each time she traveled with US combat troops. She wore protective gear that included a flak jacket, a helmet, and sometimes a gas mask, which she carried along with her cameras, lenses, and other photography equipment. Her work documenting the effects of wars and other violence is both frightening and physically challenging.

Cheryl's interest in photojournalism began in the city of Duluth, Minnesota, where she'd moved with her parents as a teenager in 1981. (She was born in the Philippines.) A friend in college was taking a photography class and brought Cheryl into the darkroom to see the process. "I was absolutely mesmerized," she said. She began studying the work of "street photographers," who chronicle life as it unfolds instead of staging shots like portraits. "Photojournalism uses photographs to tell stories, to inform, to educate—so truth is held in utmost sanctity," she said. "Photojournalists should not interfere with the integrity of the scene or the photo." Instead, she said, the photographer should act as "an observer and a witness."

Cheryl's career has taken her to places of conflict throughout the world, including war zones in Iraq and Afghanistan. She was among a very small number of female journalists in those countries, and she saw firsthand that women were not treated equally. She has become known internationally for her photos of women facing adversity.

Cheryl recognizes that photojournalism is changing rapidly because of technology and new forms of media. "I am passionate about telling stories through photography, and I will continue to do so regardless of how the format changes," she said. She encourages young people to pursue jobs in journalism, "Because although these are painfully challenging times, you will know no other job more fulfilling and adventuresome."

* Cheryl's first job in photojournalism was as a summer intern at the Minneapolis *Star Tribune* newspaper. That led to a full-time job.

* Cheryl was one of the first journalists to cover the initial days of the recent wars in Afghanistan and Iraq.

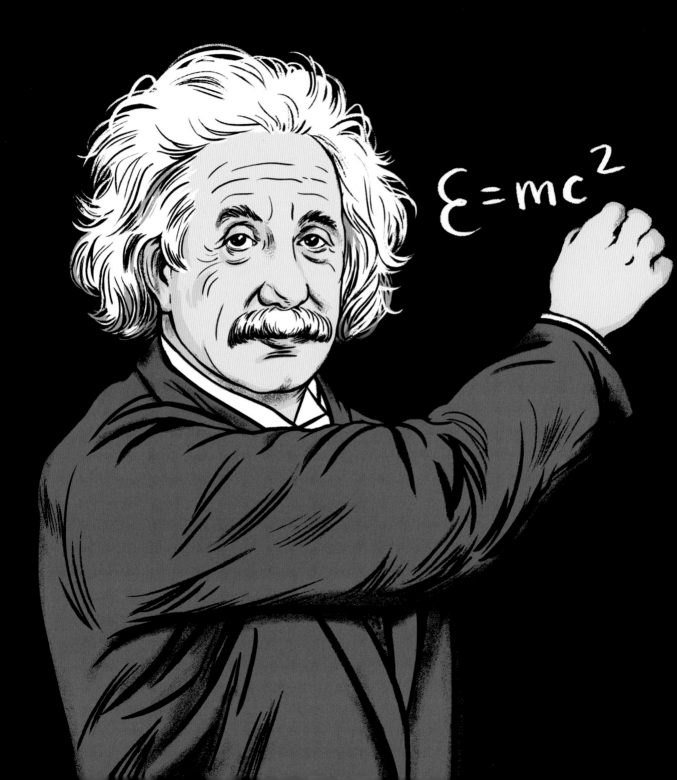

ALBERT EINSTEIN

"BLIND RESPECT FOR AUTHORITY IS THE GREATEST ENEMY OF TRUTH."

By the time Albert Einstein took refuge in the United States, he was already considered the most brilliant scientist of the twentieth century, and maybe the smartest ever. He'd transformed the way scientists think about the universe and the speed of light, and he'd won the Nobel Prize in Physics. So why did he flee to Princeton, New Jersey, in 1933?

Albert was Jewish, and his native Germany was no longer safe for Jewish people. Although World War II was several years away, Adolf Hitler was in power, and he and his Nazi Party were planning to round up and kill Jewish people. Albert, who was respected throughout the world, often visited the United States to lecture about his famous discoveries. For this, Hitler accused him of treason, his house was ransacked, and Nazis burned his books. His name was published in a German magazine as an enemy of the country, putting his life in danger.

When Albert and other Jewish scientists were forced out of their German university jobs, Albert returned to the United States to teach at the Institute for Advanced Study. He also became a US citizen. "I am privileged by fate to live here in Princeton," he wrote. "Into this small university town the chaotic voices of human strife barely penetrate. I am almost ashamed to be living in such a place while all the rest struggle and suffer."

Albert knew that his scientific discoveries about energy and matter had the potential to do harm if used in the wrong way. Near the start of World War II, he wrote to President Franklin D. Roosevelt about his concern that the Germans would develop "extremely powerful bombs of a new type." He knew Hitler might use a nuclear bomb, so he reluctantly recommended that the United States begin similar research into how to create one. Albert hoped that such weapons would never be used. He later said that a major regret in his life was that the United States dropped nuclear bombs on Japan.

Along with his wife, Elsa, Albert worked to get Jewish people out of Germany, writing visa applications and vouching for refugees who fled from Nazi rule. Joining forces with artists and political leaders, he launched the International Relief Association to assist Germans who were suffering under Hitler. Today that group is known as the International Rescue Committee and its mission has expanded to places all around the world, keeping Albert's work for refugees alive.

* Albert was strongly against racism. He joined the Princeton branch of the National Association for the Advancement of Colored People (NAACP) and worked for civil rights.

* Throughout his life, he played the violin while thinking about problems that stumped him.

KAHLIL GIBRAN

"YOU GIVE BUT LITTLE WHEN YOU GIVE OF YOUR POSSESSIONS. IT IS WHEN YOU GIVE OF YOURSELF THAT YOU TRULY GIVE."

Kahlil Gibran was born in Greater Syria (now Lebanon) in 1883, and grew up to become one of the world's best-loved poets. Only William Shakespeare and Lao Tzu have sold more books of poetry, and they had head starts of several centuries!

As a little boy, Kahlil enjoyed the peacefulness of nature. He'd tear off his clothes and stand joyfully in the pouring rain. He also loved to draw. But his household was a troubled place because of his father's heavy drinking, so his mother left her husband and brought their four children to America. They settled in a crowded Boston ghetto filled with immigrants from several countries.

Kahlil had never been to school, so he was placed in a class for students who didn't speak English. But he still managed to thrive in his busy city neighborhood, where he began taking art lessons. Sadly, when Kahlil was in his teens, his brother and one of his sisters died of tuberculosis, and his mother soon died of cancer. His remaining sister believed in Kahlil's talent and gave him money to live on while he worked on his paintings and wrote stories and poems.

A teacher named Mary Haskell admired Kahlil's work. She paid his rent later in life when he moved to a tiny apartment in New York City. They wrote long letters back and forth, and Haskell edited Kahlil's poems and stories. Another poet nicknamed Kahlil "the prophet," which he used as the title of his most famous book. In it, Kahlil imagined a holy man who had lived far from his homeland but was finally returning to his birth country. *The Prophet*'s prose poems are written as advice from this holy man about work, love, and family. Kahlil said that the theme of the book is "you are far greater than you know—and all is well."

Kahlil wrote *The Prophet* in the simple one-room apartment where he lived his entire adult life. Millions of people have turned to his poems for inspiration, comfort, and wisdom. He believed that immigrants should contribute fully to their new country without turning away from their roots. In a poem for his fellow Arab Americans, he wrote, "I believe that you have inherited from your forefathers an ancient dream, a song, a prophecy, which you can proudly lay as a gift of gratitude upon the lap of America."

* *The Prophet* gained a huge following during the counterculture "hippie" movement of the 1960s because of its message of peace.

* Kahlil's interest in art began when his mother gave him a book of Leonardo da Vinci's drawings.

SOPHIA GROJSMAN

"PERFUME IS MEDICINE."

In Sophia Grojsman's laboratory there are no white coats or microscopes. Instead the room is cluttered with hundreds of bottles containing potent smells. Sophia mixes and dabs these liquids onto blotting papers with an eyedropper, then sniffs. As the world's leading perfumer, the clever chemist has created best-selling fragrances for big-name designers.

Born in Belarus, a Soviet republic, just after World War II, Sophia didn't have toys to play with as a child, so she spent her time smelling the flowers blooming in the fields near her home. "My mother would say, 'Which flower is this?'" Sophia recalled. And Sophia would tell her. Soon, she identified a flower not by the look of its petals but by its scent.

In school, Sophia preferred chemistry, math, and cooking. She liked blending lemons and unlikely spices to create aromas her family loved to sniff. She studied in Poland, earning a degree in chemistry. But when she moved with her family to Brooklyn, New York, twenty-year-old Sophia couldn't find a job in a laboratory. She cleaned apartments for a year until a friend suggested she work at International Flavors & Fragrances. Sophia took a "nose" test and passed with flying colors, becoming an assistant to the company's perfumers.

That was in the 1970s, when most of the noses who created perfumes were men. But Sophia wasn't intimidated. She had her own theory about how to excel: "To be a perfumer you have to be a person that loves people," she said. Sophia also loved flowers and displayed her passion for them by wearing lipstick the color of pink roses and by dyeing her hair in bold stripes to mimic white freesias and black orchids.

Confident in her nose and her understanding of flowers, Sophia kept mixing and measuring ingredients to bring her own invented fragrances to life. But instead of combining hundreds of compounds as many perfumers did, Sophia focused on just a few essences. "I create small chords and put them together to make a bigger composition," she explained, comparing her work to music. Her blends created new, purer "notes" (layers of fragrance), and she became the most famous nose in the industry.

Sophia's belief in the power of perfume is simple: "When you put something around your neck that smells so good, all of a sudden you feel happy."

★ Sophia is known as the Picasso of Perfumery because "I make shorter, more concise formulas than anyone else!"

★ Most of Sophia's perfumes contain rose, which she loves.

★ Sophia also has a strong sense of taste. Growing up without refrigeration, she helped her mother with the food shopping by taste-testing the market foods for freshness.

MAZIE HIRONO

"I WANTED TO DO SOMETHING WITH MY LIFE THAT WOULD HELP PEOPLE."

In 1955, seven-year-old Mazie Keiko Hirono stood with her mom and brother on the deck of a ship sailing out of Yokohama Harbor, knowing they needed to leave Japan in a hurry. Her father's problems with alcohol and gambling had made him abusive and had left his family poor and hungry. Mazie cried a lot during the trip to Hawaii because she didn't know what to expect, but she believed in her hardworking mom. "My mother was my whole world," she remembered. "I learned risk-taking from her."

By the time Mazie entered Ka'ahumanu Elementary School, her gutsy mom was working two jobs so they could afford a room to live in. The place was so tiny that Mazie, her mother, and her brother all slept sideways on one bed. Mazie wanted to help her mother, but she had a hard time learning English. Then a librarian read her a Mary Poppins book. Mazie was so eager to read more that she quickly became fluent in her new language. She then convinced the school to let her work as a cashier in the cafeteria to earn lunch money. "I had responsibilities at home that other kids didn't have," Mazie said. "I was a serious kid."

She was also serious about helping people. While studying psychology at the University of Hawaii at Manoa, she volunteered at a YWCA to help teens struggling with drug addiction. Mazie thought she'd become a counselor and live a quiet life after her stormy childhood. But the Vietnam War changed her mind. She didn't think the United States should be involved in the war and protested with many others about it, then decided to become a lawyer to change laws and policies.

As part of her studies at the Georgetown University Law Center, Mazie read a book about feminism and the power of women to stand up for their rights. She realized that she was a risk-taker like her mother, and she decided to become a politician. Mazie won a seat in the Hawaii House of Representatives. She improved workers' rights and preschool education, and she once joined a picket line with striking schoolteachers.

In 2012, Mazie became the first Asian American woman elected to the US Senate. Wearing her favorite orchid lei, she was sworn in without a Bible, Quran, or Torah, since she was also the first Buddhist senator. "It's about time that we have people of other backgrounds and faiths in Congress," she said. Today, Senator Hirono encourages girls to get involved in politics and to vote. She still loves reading, too, and keeps stacks of books by her bedside table.

* Mazie became a US citizen in 1959—the same year Hawaii became a US state.

* Soon after Mazie's family moved to Hawaii, they lived in a one-room shack with no bathroom. They bathed outside in a large bucket.

* Growing up, Mazie kept a baseball-shaped piggy bank and filled it with dimes. Her mom often relied on the money in the bank to buy food.

FATIMAH HUSSEIN

"SOMETHING AS SIMPLE AS CLOTHING SHOULDN'T KEEP GIRLS FROM SPORTS."

Fatimah Hussein and her family escaped from a civil war in the country of Somalia when she was six years old. She and her sister joined a softball team in their new city of Minneapolis, Minnesota, which helped them adjust to life as refugees in the United States. But sports grew difficult as Fatimah got older. Like many Muslim girls and women, she and her sister covered their entire bodies when outside their homes. The skirts, long-sleeved shirts, and headscarves made Fatimah hot and uncomfortable when she played basketball and ran track. And girls were not encouraged to play sports as much as boys were.

As a young adult, Fatimah volunteered at a recreation center for Muslim kids in her neighborhood. Boys dominated the basketball court, while most girls stayed in the library or the computer lab. Fatimah knew that one way girls can feel more confident and do better in school is by playing sports, so she began to schedule hours in the gym for girls only.

But there was a problem: "Culturally appropriate athletic clothes didn't exist," Fatimah said. So she and her young athletes met with students and teachers from the University of Minnesota, working to create comfortable knee-length tunics and matching legwear. They also needed safe and breathable head coverings. Traditional coverings—known as hijabs—are made of heavy fabric and can unravel during sports action.

Fatimah contacted a tailor. They tried eighty different fabrics and many styles before developing a form-fitting, sweat-wicking hijab. It has a built-in headband to keep it secure. With a marketing professional named Jamie Glover, Fatimah then started a company called Asiya. She knew that her sports hijab could benefit many more girls than just those in her community. Minnesota state senator Kari Dziedzic connected Fatimah and Jamie with businesswomen who helped guide them toward establishing the company, and Asiya won the 2016 Minnesota Cup competition as the best women-led and minority-led business idea.

Fatimah finds great joy in seeing Muslim girls in her neighborhood on sports fields and courts. "When girls are playing, the way they smile and the way they build relationships with one another just makes me happy," she said. "Your religion and your clothes should not prevent you from being physically active."

★ *Asiya* is the name of a revered woman in Islamic history. Asiya bint Muzahim was known for her courage and for standing up to injustice.

★ Fatimah has a master's degree in social work and has spent many years working on behalf of immigrants and the elderly.

RAZIA JAN

"KNOWLEDGE IS SOMETHING NOBODY CAN STEAL."

Razia Jan lived a quiet life in Duxbury, Massachusetts, until terrorists attacked the United States on September 11, 2001. The attack was led by the group called al-Qaeda, which was based in Afghanistan. Since Razia was born in that country, people kept asking her why America had been targeted. She said she had no idea. "Afghanistan is just like a pot that has spilt over because of war. . . . It's a different culture now from when I was young; it's absolutely another world."

Growing up in the city of Kandahar in the 1950s, Razia played in the pomegranate orchards on her grandfather's farm. She went to school and wore whatever she liked, without having to cover her hair, face, or ankles like all Muslim women must do in Afghanistan today. She traveled to the United States in the 1970s to study, planning to return home afterward. But then the Soviet Union invaded Afghanistan, and Razia stayed in Massachusetts and opened a tailor shop and dry-cleaning business.

The attack on September 11 changed her focus from businesswoman to activist. Razia rallied her town to sew more than four hundred blankets for rescue workers at Ground Zero, where planes had been flown into the World Trade Center buildings in New York City. A year later, while sending care packages to US troops in Afghanistan, Razia learned that Afghan girls and women had become second-class citizens with no rights. "Their freedom was taken away," she said.

When Razia discovered that girls were forbidden to go to school and were forced into child marriages instead, she raised enough money to build a free school for girls outside of Kabul. Convincing the male elders from the villages around the city that they should let their daughters attend was difficult, but the Zabuli Education Center for Girls opened in 2008. None of the girls attending—from kindergarten through high school—could read. Even more shocking was the danger they faced just for going to class. That year, more than one hundred girls and teachers in Afghanistan were killed by terrorists who were trying to stop girls from learning.

More than six hundred girls were brave enough to attend the Zabuli school, eager to learn. "I have proved to the men . . . that this is the best thing that's happened for their daughters—to become educated," Razia said. Because of her determination, a new generation of Afghan girls has gained the power to make choices and to change the mind-sets of their communities.

* Working with the US military's Operation Shoe Fly, Razia delivered more than thirty thousand pairs of shoes to Afghan children in need.

* Razia's handmade quilts have been on display at the Pentagon, Madison Square Garden, and firehouses in New York and Massachusetts.

* In 2017, with the support of the village elders, Razia opened a women's college next to the Zabuli Education Center for Girls.

MOTHER JONES

"I HOPE I LIVE LONG ENOUGH TO BE THE GREAT-GRANDMOTHER OF ALL AGITATORS."

Mary Harris was baptized a Roman Catholic in Cork, Ireland, in 1837, though no record of her birth exists. Her farming family survived the Irish Potato Famine, but their suffering meant threadbare clothing and starvation. The Harrises fled to Canada, where Mary trained as a teacher and dressmaker at a Toronto school. She later moved to Memphis, Tennessee, married ironworker George Jones, and had four children. Then tragedy struck: Yellow fever ravaged Memphis, and Mary's husband and children died. Heartbroken, she moved to Chicago and opened a dressmaking shop.

Mary sewed elaborate gowns for Chicago's richest families, but seeing children in rags through her shop window reminded Mary of her hard life back in Ireland. When the Great Chicago Fire destroyed her business in 1871, she sought a new purpose. Walking Chicago's smoldering streets, Mary heard a speech about workers' rights. She was furious to learn about the unfair conditions miners and millworkers were forced to endure. Mary couldn't stop a famine, yellow fever, or a fire, but she could fight to make the lives of Americans better.

She traveled the country, rallying workers and organizing unions. "I reside wherever there is a good fight against wrong," she explained. Mary's fiery speeches motivated coal miners, railroad workers, and their families to protest for safer conditions, an eight-hour workday, and livable wages. If their protests didn't succeed, she urged them to strike.

But factories didn't want their workers to organize and form unions, and they fought back against Mary and her activists. She wore a hat trimmed with felt flowers and a black dress to blend in with the night as bullets fired by union opponents whizzed past her. She was locked in jail many times. Workers fondly nicknamed her Mother Jones for the risks she took on their behalf. Factory and mine owners agreed that she was "the most dangerous woman in America."

Mother Jones wasn't intimidated by threats and powerful men—not even the president of the United States. In 1903, when she learned of children sewing in factories instead of going to school, she led a children's march to President Teddy Roosevelt's front door. Roosevelt didn't answer, but news generated by the march helped end child labor.

Nearly one hundred years after she was born, Mother Jones still spoke out. Her explosive words rallied millions of workers half her age to march against injustice. She refused to believe that money, gender, or age had anything to do with accomplishing great things. Even today, her courage lives on at every labor rally and union meeting in America.

* *Mother Jones*, a progressive magazine started in 1976 and now a website, was named after Mother Mary Harris Jones. The website has eleven million monthly readers.

* May 1 is International Workers' Day and the chosen birthday of Mother Jones.

* Mother Jones started the first labor union that included women and workers of all races.

MEB KEFLEZIGHI

"WINNING THE BOSTON MARATHON IS THE MOST MEANINGFUL VICTORY IN MY LIFETIME."

Meb Keflezighi was born in the war-torn African country of Eritrea. His village had no electricity or running water, and food was scarce. Sometimes Meb and his ten brothers and sisters ate dirt to soothe their hunger. "You just dig deep [in] the ground, until you feel the moisture," he said. "Whatever you needed to do to survive."

The Red Cross helped the Keflezighi family flee to Italy, and from there they came to the United States as refugees. Meb was twelve when they arrived in California on October 21, 1987. "It's like a birthday for us," he said about the date. "I take so much pride in being an American." Meb's father worked as a janitor and drove a cab. The kids learned English by studying a dictionary, and all of them earned college degrees. Meb graduated from the University of California, Los Angeles, where he became an international running star.

In 2013, Meb cheered as the Boston Marathon leaders raced past him to the finish line. Though he was one of the world's fastest marathoners, Meb didn't compete that day. Shortly after he left the finish-line area, two bombs exploded nearby, injuring more than two hundred sixty-three people and killing three. Meb was shocked that terrorists had struck one of America's greatest sports events.

A year after the bombing, Meb lined up at the start of the 2014 Boston Marathon. As a US citizen and a former refugee, he was eager to win, making a statement that the terrorist attack would not tarnish this great American tradition. But no US runner had won the race in thirty years. Meb carried extra motivation: He'd written the names of the victims killed in the bombing on the number he wore on his jersey.

As he took the lead, Meb kept thinking *Boston strong, Meb strong.* He extended his lead to nearly a minute, but then a pair of runners from Kenya began to close the gap. The crowds chanted Meb's name and "U-S-A" as he fought to stay in front. He thought about the victims of the bombing for strength. "They helped carry me through," he said after crossing the finish line—the winner of an unforgettable race. Meb kissed the ground three times and began to cry. "As an athlete, you have dreams, and today is where dream and reality meet."

Meb earned a silver medal at the 2004 Olympic Games. He has represented the United States in the Olympics four times.

The Meb Foundation is devoted to children's health, education, and fitness.

Before every race, Meb eats *himbasha* bread, freshly baked by his mother, Awetash. It reminds him of the strength of his ancestors.

YO-YO MA

"WHENEVER TWO CULTURES MEET, IT'S THE LITTLE THINGS THAT MAKE A BIG DIFFERENCE."

Yo-Yo Ma was born in Paris, France, to Chinese parents. He learned to play German classical music on an Italian cello. Surrounded by so many cultures growing up, it's no surprise that he is famous for blending music from around the world into new classical sounds.

Music had always been a part of Yo-Yo Ma's family. His mother was a singer and his violinist father taught music at China's Nanjing University. In 1958, at age three, Yo-Yo picked up his first instrument, the violin. He decided to be a cello player by the time he was four. When he moved with his family to New York City three years later, Yo-Yo was already a famous musician. He played for presidents Dwight D. Eisenhower and John F. Kennedy and was featured on television, performing with his sister under the famous conductor Leonard Bernstein.

Being expected to play perfectly and beautifully all the time meant getting up before five in the morning every day to practice. "As a younger person and as an immigrant, you feel a lot of pressure," Yo-Yo recalled about his training. By the time he graduated from the music program at the Juilliard School, Yo-Yo wanted to learn something other than music. He attended Harvard University to study anthropology and German literature.

After college, Yo-Yo was eager to pick up the cello again, but everything changed when he was diagnosed with severe scoliosis. He had surgery to correct the curvature of his spine and had to wear a body cast. No one knew if he'd be able to be a world-class musician again, but he recovered and his career took off. Calling himself "tri-cultural" as a Paris-born Chinese American, Yo-Yo Ma pursued his lifelong interest in how music affects people and how people affect music.

He mixed tango music with classical compositions and worked with jazz artist Bobby McFerrin to perform lullabies. Yo-Yo loved the fusion of these world sounds so much, he started the Silkroad Project. In this group, musicians gather from around the globe to create music on instruments once popular on the Silk Road trade route thousands of years ago. They perform on the Galician bagpipe, the Korean *jang-go* drum, the Mongolian horsehead fiddle, and of course, Yo-Yo performs on his Italian cello.

"Everything that I've experienced as a cellist, as a traveling musician, as an immigrant . . ." Yo-Yo explained, "has made me think about cultural connectors."

★ Yo-Yo Ma has won more than fifteen Grammy Awards, performed on movie soundtracks, and jammed on *Sesame Street*.

★ His cello, made by the famous Domenico Montagnana in 1733, is worth nearly three million dollars. A student called it "Petunia," and Yo-Yo Ma kept the nickname.

★ *Yo* means "friendship" in Chinese.

MARYAM MIRZAKHANI

"I FIND IT FASCINATING THAT YOU CAN LOOK AT THE SAME PROBLEM FROM DIFFERENT PERSPECTIVES."

Women have been blazing trails in science and mathematics for centuries, but they've rarely been given credit for it. Iranian-born mathematician Maryam Mirzakhani helped change that. She solved math problems that seemed impossible and that had stumped scientists for hundreds of years. Math masters consider her one of the great mathematicians of this century.

But there was nothing great about Maryam's school days in the city of Tehran during the 1980s, as war raged between the countries of Iran and Iraq. Luckily, the fighting ended in time for Maryam to attend middle school, but the brilliant thinker had little interest in numbers. Walking past a row of bookstores on her way to class, she instead fell in love with stories. "I dreamt of becoming a writer," she admitted. Then one day her brother described to Maryam how a young student had ingeniously found a way to rapidly add up all the numbers from 1 to 100. Maryam was fascinated. "The more time I spent on mathematics, the more excited I became."

Maryam attended an all-girls high school where she learned about scientist Marie Curie, who won Nobel Prizes in both physics and chemistry. Inspired by a woman who excelled in fields dominated by men, Maryam convinced her principal to provide her classmates with the same challenging math lessons that boys received at other schools. At seventeen, Maryam and her best friend became the first girls to compete for Team Iran at the International Mathematical Olympiad. Maryam won the competition two years in a row, the second time with a perfect score.

After studying at Sharif University in Tehran, Maryam came to the United States to attend graduate school at Harvard University. Then she began teaching at Stanford, and she eventually solved a complex problem in hyperbolic geometry, which is a kind of math that measures and finds equations for curved surfaces like billiard balls and doughnut shapes. For this, in 2014, she became the first woman to be awarded the Fields Medal, considered the Nobel Prize in math. Though she died of breast cancer at age forty, Maryam is a role model for future mathematicians and has become the Marie Curie of the twenty-first century.

* Doodling helped Maryam stay focused on difficult math problems. She constantly drew on huge pieces of paper scattered on the floor of her home office.

* Maryam remained best friends with Roya Beheshti Zavareh, who competed with her at the International Mathematical Olympiad. Dr. Beheshti Zavareh is a math professor at Washington University in St. Louis.

JOHN MUIR

"THE WINDS WILL BLOW THEIR OWN FRESHNESS INTO YOU, AND THE STORMS THEIR ENERGY."

John Muir didn't have much spare time growing up. His father was so strict that he rarely let John hike the Scottish countryside after school or between chores. But John figured out a way to be "wild" in nature: He climbed onto the roof at night and stared at the stars while the wind ruffled his nightshirt.

John slept even less after his family immigrated to the United States when he was ten years old. His father made him work long hours on the family farm in Wisconsin instead of going to school. Determined to learn, John spent nights teaching himself algebra and geometry. He even invented alarm clocks so other people could make the most of their time, too, and he sold his inventions to pay for his schooling at the University of Wisconsin.

But for John, nothing compared with being outdoors. In 1867, after he took a job in a wagon-wheel factory and a piece of flying metal blinded him, John made himself a promise: If his eyesight returned, he'd spend the rest of his life in nature. A few months later he could see again, and he started a lengthy trek from Kentucky to Florida, going "anywhere that is wild," jotting notes and pressing flowers in a notebook he titled *John Muir, Earth-planet, Universe.*

Years later, in the Sierra Nevada mountains, John grew sad watching humans chop down forests that were thousands of years old. He decided that someone had to save America's natural beauty or it would be wiped out. John became an environmentalist, and he worked hard to convince lawmakers to pass bills turning precious land into protected national parks. John even hiked in Yosemite National Park with President Teddy Roosevelt and convinced him that the best way to preserve the park was to have the federal government manage it.

Flowers, butterflies, and hiking trails all over the United States are named after John Muir, and his books inspire people around the world to take the time to enjoy nature. But it was his deep connection to the land that ensured millions of acres of treasured American landscape are kept wild in the US National Park Service.

* John cofounded the Sierra Club, which preserves land and defends the legacy of America's national parks.

* He invented a bed alarm clock that literally got him out of bed. The alarm was hooked to the end of the bedpost and jolted him upright at the set time.

* John's radical theory that glaciers carved out mountains and valleys was later proven to be true by geologists.

DIKEMBE MUTOMBO

"IT'S GOOD TO BE FAMOUS BY PLAYING THE GAME OF BASKETBALL. BUT WHAT ARE YOU DOING WITH IT? WHAT ARE YOU DOING WITH THE FAME AND THE SKILL?"

Dikembe Mutombo thrived in the NBA for eighteen seasons, but his success didn't come easily. Before Dikembe became a basketball star, his college teammate Alonzo Mourning used to overpower him every day in practice, constantly dunking the ball. Coach John Thompson told Dikembe he needed to get tougher. But Dikembe hadn't played much basketball while growing up in the African country of Zaire (now the Democratic Republic of the Congo [DRC]). In fact, he'd earned a scholarship to Georgetown University for academics, not sports.

Dikembe spoke nine languages but only a little English when he arrived in the United States, and he'd never played basketball before he was sixteen years old. "Dikembe didn't know how to play, but [he] hustled," Coach Thompson said. He knew Dikembe's seven-foot two-inch height would be a huge asset if he worked on his skills, and eventually his hard work made him a scoring, rebounding, and shot-blocking standout.

After his strong college career, the Denver Nuggets chose Dikembe with the fourth pick in the 1991 NBA draft. As one of the league's top defenders, Dikembe developed his trademark finger wagging and his "Not in my house!" roar after swatting away shots by Michael Jordan and other stars. But basketball wasn't Dikembe's only passion. "I come from a society that is very poor, very abandoned," he said.

Basketball made him wealthy and famous, but he always remembered the proverb his mother used to say to him: *When you take the elevator up to reach the top, please don't forget to send it down.* So Dikembe led humanitarian efforts around the world, raising money and awareness for treating polio, AIDS, and malaria, and assisting with women's health issues in his home country.

Dikembe's proudest achievement is the Biamba Marie Mutombo Hospital—named for his mother—in the capital city of Kinshasa. He donated most of the thirty million dollars needed to build the hospital, which was the first one constructed in the DRC in forty years. For his efforts, he was named the world's most generous athlete.

During a ceremony in Dikembe's honor, the NBA commissioner said, "You were born in the Congo but you are a true American success story. . . . You've done more than any player that I can think of."

* Dikembe's full name is Dikembe Mutombo Mpolondo Mukamba Jean-Jacques Wamutombo.

* His shoe size is twenty-two!

* Dikembe retired with the second-most blocked shots in NBA history.

MARTINA NAVRATILOVA

"LABELS ARE FOR CLOTHING. LABELS ARE NOT FOR PEOPLE."

When Martina Navratilova was a kid, she loved hitting tennis balls against a wall and eating spinach because she thought it would give her muscles like Popeye. What she didn't like was waiting in line to buy bread and milk in Czechoslovakia (now the Czech Republic)—or that her parents had been kicked out of the university they attended because they'd spoken out against the Communist government.

A short, scrawny kid who was "all ears and feet," Martina focused on sports. She always knew she'd become a tennis star. It helped that her stepdad thought so, too. "He would hit the ball to me for hours, telling me I would be a great champion," she said. After Martina won the Czech national championship and the government took control of her career, she also knew she'd have to find a way to leave Czechoslovakia.

At eighteen years old, Martina lost in the 1975 US Open semifinals to Chris Evert. But playing in the tournament gave her the opportunity she needed, and she defected, staying in the United States and applying for American citizenship. Her decision meant that she lost her Czech citizenship and was cut off from her family.

Lonely and without a country, Martina binged on fast food. She gained twenty-five pounds, slowing her speed and endurance. But after she became a US citizen in 1981, Martina's career soared. She trained harder and showed the world who she really was: a champion. She also became one of the first sports stars to announce that she is gay.

Back then, athletes knew coming out as gay could end their careers. Some companies stopped sponsoring Martina, and people booed her at matches. But she knew there was nothing wrong with being a lesbian or with being honest. "My sexuality doesn't matter," Martina said. "Nor does where I'm from, that I'm left-handed, or that I'm a woman."

Fans soon agreed. They loved watching her compete against Chris Evert, who became Martina's main rival on the court and also a good friend. Martina went on to win more tournaments than any player in history and hoisted the Wimbledon trophy a record nine times. When people thought she was too old to keep winning, she switched to doubles and became the oldest champion of a Grand Slam tournament. "The ball doesn't know how old you are," she said. Today Martina still speaks her mind, encouraging businesses to reflect the real world by being more diverse.

* Martina won fifty-nine Grand Slam tennis tournaments in singles, doubles, and mixed doubles.

* Growing up, Martina loved watching American movies with feisty women characters played by actress Katharine Hepburn.

* Martina waited until she was a United States citizen before coming out, because an immigration law back then discriminated against gay people. She could have been deported.

INDRA NOOYI

"I HAVE NEVER SHIED AWAY FROM THE FACT THAT I AM AN INDIAN AND I DON'T INTEND TO, BUT YOU CAN BE AT HOME WITH BOTH CULTURES."

Indra Krishnamurthy Nooyi grew up as the middle child in a traditional Tamil household in Chennai, India. Her mother devoted her time to the kids while Indra's dad traveled a lot as a banker. But Indra wasn't a traditional Indian girl. She played cricket on an all-girls team and strummed rock tunes on her guitar.

Like her siblings, Indra was expected to be a little like both her parents and to earn perfect grades. Her mom prayed for hours asking that Indra do well in school. "She always said to us, 'I want to get you married when you are eighteen, and make sure you aspire to be the prime minister,'" Indra explained. But Indra did neither. Her grandfather encouraged her to be whoever she wanted and helped convince Indra's mom that Indra should choose her own path.

In 1978, after graduating from the Indian Institute of Management, she earned a scholarship to Yale University and answered telephones at night as a dorm receptionist. Indra worked harder than anyone during summer internships, where her managers noticed how her fresh ideas resulted in increased sales. "I could see the world through the eyes of people from outside the United States," Indra said about her many strengths. She also maintained her Indian traditions, like praying to Ganesh—the Hindu god of success—and eating vegetarian food.

Using her analytical mind to discover how companies work best, Indra became the chief strategist at PepsiCo and proposed a radical idea for the company to branch out beyond soda. Sales skyrocketed. Twelve years later, Indra was the first woman and the first Hindu to be named PepsiCo's CEO (chief executive officer). She's up before the sun rises and is constantly trying to balance family and work time. "Trust me, I haven't done everything right," she said. But "to be a CEO is a calling. . . .I love the job."

Indra's persistence, work ethic, and international outlook have transformed a billion-dollar American company, proving that no matter who you are or where you come from, you can achieve great things.

* Indra likes to hum out loud while she's working and says she has music running through her mind all day.

* She played guitar in an all-woman rock band.

* She loves the game of cricket, but in the United States she discovered baseball. She became a fan of the New York Yankees.

53

ADRIANA OCAMPO

"SPACE EXPLORATION WAS MY PASSION FROM A VERY YOUNG AGE, AND I KNEW I WANTED TO BE A PART OF IT."

When she was a little girl, Adriana Ocampo climbed to the roof of her home in Argentina and imagined that there could be life in outer space. "I couldn't go to sleep in the evening without looking at the stars and wondering what those little points of light were," she said. Adriana built spaceships from her mother's pots and pans, and she dressed her dolls in space suits. Taurus, the family dog, served as her tail-wagging copilot. She dreamed of building colonies on other worlds and learned everything she could about the science of space travel.

In 1969, Adriana watched astronauts walk on the moon for the first time on her television. Fascinated by the moon's unusual soil and rocks, she decided that she wanted to study other planets. So when her family moved to the United States a year later, fifteen-year-old Adriana's first question was "Where is NASA?" She learned to speak English in a hurry and landed a summer job at the National Aeronautics and Space Administration's Jet Propulsion Laboratory. Her imagination and hours of studying were already paying off.

Adriana was excited to be surrounded by scientists who were unlocking the mysteries of space exploration. But something was missing: other women and other Latinx. "I couldn't see a reflection of me," Adriana said. That didn't stop her; she continued to work at NASA while earning her degrees, and in her career as a planetary geologist, she has led NASA's probes of Jupiter, Venus, Mars, Pluto, and the asteroids.

Closer to home, Adriana's research led to the discovery of the Chicxulub impact crater in Mexico. The crater was caused by a six-mile-wide asteroid crashing into the Earth millions of years ago, and its worldwide effects killed off the dinosaurs. Adriana's crater exploration grew from another of her childhood passions: "It is the dream of every child to play in the dirt. We geologists get to do it for real."

In 2016, Adriana Ocampo was named the National Hispanic Scientist of the Year. She hopes that honor will inspire more Latinas to pursue careers in science. "I was raised to believe you could do anything you wanted with effort, time, and persistence," she tells students. She loves the opportunities that being an American has opened for her, and she knows from her own experience that newcomers to the United States bring great ideas and energy. "This is why I always love telling everybody at NASA that I am an immigrant," she said.

★ Adriana was born in Colombia, but her parents soon moved to Buenos Aires, Argentina.

★ She was among the first humans to see the surface of Mars when NASA's *Viking* lander sent photos back to Earth.

PAULINE PARK

"WE OUGHT TO BE JUDGED NOT ONLY BY HOW WE TRY TO HELP THOSE WHO ARE LIKE US, BUT ALSO BY HOW WE TRY TO HELP THOSE WHO ARE DIFFERENT FROM US."

Pauline Park says she was destined to question identity. Born a Korean boy in 1960, she was adopted by a European American couple, along with her twin brother. They were the only nonwhite kids in her Milwaukee neighborhood.

Pauline knew she wouldn't grow up looking like her parents, but after her first day of kindergarten she also knew she didn't feel like a boy. She was born with male body parts but identified as a girl. "I knew that I was transgendered when I was five years old," Pauline explained. In the 1960s, she had no idea there was a word for this. In fact, the term *transgender* (not identifying with the sex you are born with) was only first used in 1965, while Pauline was in kindergarten. She came home from school and asked her mom to buy her stirrup pants like the other girls wore, and her mom was astonished. She told Pauline that she was a boy. Though Pauline didn't want to, she decided to keep her identity a secret.

She grew older, enjoying opera music that she borrowed from the library and performing in the orchestra in high school. "Playing the piano . . . sustained me through many ups and downs," she said. She earned three university degrees and studied German in a twelfth-century medieval tower in Germany. But Pauline longed to live her life as a woman. "There was never any time I wasn't aware of being different," she said.

By age thirty-six she felt confident enough to wear women's clothes and to change her name to Pauline. But it wasn't until she moved to New York City that Pauline became an activist, fighting for freedom of gender identity and expression. She convinced gay and lesbian advocacy groups to include transgender people under the title LGBT (lesbian, gay, bisexual, transgender). Pauline also wanted to make sure transgender people couldn't be bullied or denied work, and she pushed for a transgender rights bill to be part of New York City's human rights law. In 2002, Mayor Michael Bloomberg signed the bill into law with Pauline standing next to him.

By courageously embracing her true identity and encouraging others to accept people for who they are, Pauline Park has helped transform the way society thinks about gender.

★ With nearly a million people cheering her, Pauline became the first openly transgendered person to be grand marshal of the New York City Pride March in 2005.

★ Pauline's favorite book is J. R. R. Tolkien's *The Lord of the Rings*.

I. M. PEI

"SUCCESS IS A COLLECTION OF PROBLEMS SOLVED."

When Ieoh Ming Pei was a small boy in China, his mother often took him to see gardens and shrines. A devout Buddhist, she taught her son to meditate in these beautiful places, which were "wonderful marriages of man-made and natural design," I. M. recalled nearly a century later. "They are my guide."

I. M.'s mother died in 1930 when he was thirteen years old, shortly after the family had moved to the rapidly growing city of Shanghai. I. M. watched as the cityscape grew around him. His early impressions of gardens and high-rise buildings led him to a career in design, where he is known as the Master of Modern Architecture.

I. M. considered going to college in England, but decided to attend the Massachusetts Institute of Technology in Cambridge because he loved American movies with actors like Buster Keaton and Charlie Chaplin. I. M. intended to return to China after graduation, but World War II made it impossible for him to travel home. So he took a job with the US National Defense Research Committee. He then became a US citizen and started his own architectural company.

He is known for his bold use of geometric shapes, his melding of past and present elements, and his glass-and-concrete buildings. His hundreds of designs include the Rock & Roll Hall of Fame in Cleveland, the John F. Kennedy Presidential Library and Museum in Boston, and the glass pyramid at the Louvre museum in Paris. They range from the seventy-story Bank of China Tower in Hong Kong to apartment complexes throughout the United States.

I. M.'s toughest assignment, though, was designing the Museum of Islamic Art in the country of Qatar. How could he reflect centuries of Islamic art in one building? He took his inspiration from a ninth-century mosque in Cairo, Egypt, and mixed modern and ancient elements. "It is good to learn from the ancients," I. M. said. "They had a lot of time to think about architecture and landscape. Today we rush everything, but architecture is slow, and the landscapes it sits in even slower."

In 1983, I. M. was honored with the Pritzker Prize, considered the highest achievement in architecture. He used the prize money to fund scholarships for Chinese students to study architecture in the United States. A tireless, kind, and brilliant man, I. M. Pei was still designing buildings well into his nineties. "I've been active all my life," he said. On April 26, 2017, he turned 100 years old.

★ I. M. took great pride in designing the Suzhou Museum, since his ancestors had lived in that Chinese city for hundreds of years. He spent summers there when he was a child.

★ Two of I. M.'s four children became architects like their dad.

JORGE RAMOS

"THE UNITED STATES GAVE ME OPPORTUNITIES THAT MY COUNTRY OF ORIGIN COULD NOT: FREEDOM OF THE PRESS AND COMPLETE FREEDOM OF EXPRESSION."

On the day Jorge Ramos crossed the Rio Grande, the river's waters were dark and polluted, with heavy muck churning in the current. Jorge swam swiftly between Laredo, Texas, and Nuevo Laredo, Mexico, knowing that many had drowned trying to cross that stretch. People from Mexico and Central America sometimes cross the Rio Grande illegally, desperate to reach the safety, freedom, and opportunities of the United States. Many of them are kids. "It's incredibly dangerous," Jorge said. "There are very strong undercurrents, a lot of rocks and plants, and a muddy bottom. . . . Imagine what it is like at night for these children." Jorge, one of the world's best-known television journalists, made the swim in 2014 to call attention to the reasons people flee their countries.

His own entry to the United States in 1983 was easier. He'd been working as a TV reporter in Mexico City, where he grew up. But his bosses and Mexican officials rejected his reports that were critical of the government. Fed up, Jorge sold his car so he could buy a plane ticket to Los Angeles. "I had a student visa, and I remember thinking, *This is freedom.*"

Jorge found a job as a reporter with a TV station in LA. He now anchors the news for Noticiero Univision, writes influential books and a newspaper column, and provides daily radio commentary. He's known as the Voice of the Voiceless for his support of the rights of immigrants and for telling their stories. "The really, really good journalists always take a stand with those who have no power, with those who have no rights, and with those who have no voice," he said.

Jorge asks tough questions. He often challenged President Barack Obama about his immigration policies during interviews at the White House. He also stood up to Donald Trump at a press conference during the 2016 presidential campaign, peppering the future president with questions on his negative comments about Mexicans. Trump repeatedly told Jorge to sit down, and a bodyguard forced Jorge out of the room. That reminded Jorge of the censorship he'd faced as a journalist in Mexico City. "It was an attack on the freedom of the press in the United States," he said. As one of the world's most influential Spanish-speaking journalists, the altercation only spurred him to fight harder in the future—for the press, for immigrants, and for all Americans.

* When Jorge arrived in the United States in 1983, he carried his guitar and little else. He still has the guitar.

* Jorge is a dual citizen of Mexico and the United States.

61

MARCUS SAMUELSSON

"WITHOUT CULTURE WE ARE NOTHING."

Born in Ethiopia during a tuberculosis epidemic, baby Kassahun Tsegie rode in his mother's arms as she and his sister walked for days to a hospital. His mother died there, but he and his sister survived. Lennart and Anne Marie Samuelsson adopted them and brought them home to Gothenburg, Sweden.

They were "the only black kids not just on the block but in school," but Kassahun—now named Marcus Samuelsson—fell in love with Swedish food and culture. On summer mornings, he loved fishing with his father for lobsters and mackerel. He became a soccer standout for one of the top youth clubs in "Gburg" and was sure he'd become a professional player. But at sixteen, he was shocked when his coach dropped him from the team. "Too small" was the verdict. He needed a new career!

Marcus had always enjoyed cooking, inspired by his grandmother Helga, who had welcomed him as a kitchen helper when he was a little boy. "There was always a season in Helga's kitchen, and I loved that," he recalled. So Marcus enrolled in culinary school and took a job at one of Gburg's hottest restaurants. He then worked his way around Europe, training with top chefs. An apprenticeship at New York City's Aquavit restaurant brought Marcus to America. He stood out as a line cook, expertly preparing pan-roasted venison and glazed salmon. In his free time he Rollerbladed and ate his way through the restaurants in Koreatown, Chinatown, and other neighborhoods, and he became more and more well-known for his cooking.

His bright personality and sense of fashion made Marcus a celebrity chef (he won the grand prize on *Top Chef Masters*), but he feels there are no shortcuts to true success. "There's two ways to get famous," he said. "There used to be one way: You worked really hard, and you were really good. . . . I still believe in that one." The path he *doesn't* admire involves instant fame, the kind you can get by doing something outrageous on TV or the Internet. "I have zero interest in that."

Marcus draws on his Swedish and Ethiopian roots to meld flavors and sees cooking as a way to bring cultures together. Today he owns about a dozen restaurants in the United States and is proud to employ hundreds of people. Many of his restaurants specialize in delicacies inspired by his grandmother's recipes. "The roasted chicken I make today is an homage to hers."

★ As a teenager, Marcus loved the music of Michael Jackson and Miles Davis.

★ In 2008, Marcus prepared the meal for President Barack Obama's first state dinner.

★ Marcus has written many bestselling cookbooks and two books about his life.

CARLOS SANTANA

"I WOULD NEVER TAKE ANYTHING FROM AMERICA THAT I WOULDN'T WANT TO PUT BACK A HUNDRED TIMES."

When Carlos Santana was nine years old, his father took out a violin and played softly. A bird settled on a branch and sang along with the instrument. "It was as if I suddenly found out my father was a great wizard," Carlos recalled, "only this wasn't magic—it was music." Carlos's father was a professional musician, and he taught his son the basics. But he was gone for weeks at a time as his mariachi band moved from city to city, so Carlos figured out how to play on his own, listening to the jazz, blues, rock 'n' roll, and traditional Mexican music that echoed around him.

The Santana family lived in a small town in Mexico, but Carlos's father had opportunities in the city of Tijuana, just below the US border, so the family moved there. Carlos sold sticks of gum to tourists to help buy groceries. He teamed up with two guitarists and earned money playing music. By the time he was fourteen he had a steady job backing adult bands in a Tijuana bar on his guitar. He was just a kid!

Carlos kept learning, listening to Caribbean salsa and American pop. He studied African American performers like Miles Davis and B. B. King. "I was teaching myself to listen, to figure out how to take a song apart and put it back together," he said. Some nights he'd perform on the guitar until six o'clock in the morning, then go straight to church and play his violin for the service.

When the family moved to San Francisco, California, Carlos formed a band. But what kind of music would they play? He realized that the best guitarists conveyed something personal through their music. "It was who they were, what they were thinking of when they played," he said. "Other bands were like copies of copies"—there was nothing original about their music. So Carlos developed his own sound.

His band, Santana, signed a record deal when Carlos was only twenty-one years old. They had huge hits like "Evil Ways" and "Black Magic Woman." When they performed in front of half a million people at the Woodstock music festival in 1969, their popularity soared. Carlos has been an international superstar ever since, with guitarists from all over the world trying to play like he does.

* In 2000, Santana's *Supernatural* won eight Grammy awards, tying Michael Jackson's *Thriller* for the most awarded for one album.

* Carlos established the Milagro Foundation to provide money to organizations that work with children around the world in education, health, and the arts.

* Carlos became an American citizen in 1965.

YASSER SEIRAWAN

"AMERICANS GRAVITATE TOWARDS CHAMPIONS— FULL STOP, END OF STORY."

The city of Seattle is famous for its coffee and its rainfall. Those two things converged to launch the career of a chess genius in 1972.

When he was four years old, Yasser Seirawan and his parents fled Syria using forged passports after a civil war broke out. They moved to England, and eventually Virginia Beach, where "Yaz" turned into a daring surfer and diver. But then he and his newly divorced mother moved to a cramped Seattle apartment, where twelve-year-old Yaz watched the record-breaking rain pour down. "I wasn't tanning, I was rusting," he said. "It just rained for weeks on end."

Yaz and a neighbor, David Chapman, spent the days indoors playing poker, chess, and other games. Even though David "spent the whole summer clobbering [him]," Yaz loved chess. "The thing that really attracted me was the individualism in it," he said. "If you lose a game, you lose it. No one else. You rely strictly on yourself." Yaz then found an even tougher opponent in Washington State champion James Harley McCormick, who often played chess at a nearby coffeehouse called The Last Exit. Yaz sharpened his game there, playing mostly against adults, and within a year he'd won the state junior championship.

A brilliant student, he graduated from high school in just three years, spending his free time swimming; playing tennis; rocking out to Michael Jackson, Supertramp, and Stevie Wonder; and devouring Isaac Asimov's science fiction. Then he took off for New York City, where he scraped by as a chess hustler, winning money in street competitions and testing his game against savvy, lightning-quick players. He also swept through official chess tournaments, and by age nineteen, he'd won the world junior title and had set his sights on his first US Open Championship. He wound up winning the US title four times before becoming a TV commentator for major competitions.

For Yaz, chess is the most exciting and nerve-wracking game on the planet. "The nervous tension! It can kill you!" he said. "A fumbled pass, a missed free throw, a netted tennis shot can't begin to compare to a bad chess move." He is now a chess ambassador who inspires young players to take up the game.

* Yaz started a chess program at his high school during his freshman year and taught the game to other students. The next year, the team won the state championship.

* Yaz was the editor of *Inside Chess* magazine for many years and has written several books about chess strategy.

NIKOLA TESLA

"MY PARAMOUNT DESIRE TODAY, WHICH GUIDES ME IN EVERYTHING I DO . . . IS TO HARNESS THE FORCES OF NATURE TO THE SERVICE OF MANKIND."

Nikola Tesla never had to look far for inspiration. His hardworking mother milked the cows on their farm in Croatia and recited lengthy poems from memory. She was a nonstop innovator, building tools and spinning clothing from her homemade thread. Little Nikola started making things, too. At age five, he created a waterwheel turned by the power of a stream. He glued bugs to a pulley to make a motor, which was powered by the bugs' flapping wings. He knocked himself unconscious when he tried to fly by jumping off a roof holding an open umbrella.

Nikola's father, on the other hand, was a minister in the Serbian Orthodox Church and very strict. He owned a room full of books that Nikola wasn't allowed to touch, so Nikola made his own candles and stayed up at night secretly reading. Soon, he'd memorized poems in English, French, German, and Italian. And he never forgot *anything* he'd learned!

One day Nikola noticed sparks flying when he stroked his cat's fur. He decided that electrical energy must be everywhere. Nikola put his incredible memory to work figuring out how to harness that energy. He imagined things that no one had come up with before. As a teenager, he pictured complex inventions in his mind and understood how they would work. "I could visualize motors and generators," he said. "The images I saw were to me perfectly real and tangible." If he saw flaws in his imaginary designs, he fixed them.

In the late 1800s, major cities were adding electrical power. American inventor Thomas Edison led the way with his development of direct current (DC) electricity. But Edison's work required generating stations to be built every mile. Nikola admired Edison, and he immigrated to the United States to work for him. But Nikola had a plan to use alternating current (AC) electricity, which he believed would cover vastly bigger areas. Nikola was part of a huge wave of immigrants from Europe and Asia who had come to work for the railroads, factories, mines, and mills that were turning the United States into an industrial giant. Nikola knew that AC power would make all of that happen faster and better.

Edison felt threatened by Nikola's plans and tried to block them. But a rival businessman believed in Nikola's ideas and hired him to power the Chicago World's Fair of 1893. The fair was a huge success and showed the world the benefits of AC, which would eventually change the American way of life. Radio, wireless technology, X-rays, and many other innovations all came about because of Nikola Tesla and his incredible ideas.

★ Nikola was obsessed with numbers divisible by three. He'd walk around a block three times before entering a building. For exercise, he'd swim twenty-seven laps around a pool. If he stayed in a hotel, his room number had to be divisible by three.

HAMDI ULUKAYA

"THE MINUTE A REFUGEE HAS A JOB, THAT'S THE MINUTE THEY STOP BEING A REFUGEE."

Growing up with six brothers on a farm in Turkey, Hamdi Ulukaya herded sheep and goats with his Kurdish family. He spent part of the year away from home, following his flocks through the mountains. He also helped his parents make feta cheese and yogurt from their animals' milk. Their thick, strained yogurt tasted so delicious that villagers gobbled it up and it became a family business.

After graduating from Ankara University in 1994, Hamdi traveled to New York and studied English at Adelphi University. Not only did he miss his family, he longed for their cheese and yogurt. Hamdi's father convinced him to make feta cheese to sell to New Yorkers. But Hamdi also wanted to make yogurt that was as thick, creamy, and naturally sweet as at home. "We grew up with this," he said. "We cannot think a meal or diet, a day without yogurt."

Hamdi read about a yogurt factory for sale in South Edmeston, New York, and took a tour. The surrounding mountains reminded him of Turkey, and he was impressed by the passion of the former workers who showed him around. Hamdi bought the factory, and his first employees were the people who had lost their jobs when the factory closed. He named his company Chobani, which comes from the Turkish word for *shepherd*. "It represents giving, kindness," Hamdi explained.

After perfecting the Ulukaya family recipe, Chobani delivered its first cases of yogurt in 2007. Hamdi's business became a huge success, and because it provided jobs for the community, it saved South Edmeston from financial ruin. But Hamdi didn't stop helping others there. While visiting the Greek island of Lesbos, he witnessed the forced migration of tens of thousands of refugees fleeing for safety. He spoke about the crisis at the World Economic Forum in Switzerland, insisting that corporations have a responsibility to support refugees by hiring them. His company employs two thousand people in the United States from diverse backgrounds, including refugees from Iraq, Afghanistan, and African countries.

Shepherding, or caring for communities, has become Hamdi's passion. As a refugee rights activist and one of the world's wealthiest people, he's pledged to give most of his money to help them. "I go to sleep feeling really good," he said. "Business is still the strongest, most effective way to change the world."

* Hamdi loves animals and his two German shepherds love eating yogurt.

* Hamdi built the world's largest yogurt factory in Twin Falls, Idaho.

* There is no record of Hamdi's exact date of birth since he was born on a mountain and not in a hospital.

ROSE WINSLOW

"WE SHALL CONTINUE TO PICKET BECAUSE IT IS OUR RIGHT."

American women would not have the right to vote without the courage of people like Rose Winslow. The words of this Polish American activist brought attention to the women's rights movement and changed history.

Born Ruza Wenclawska in Suwałki, Poland, Rose immigrated to Pennsylvania with her parents when she was a baby. As Rose grew up, her father toiled in the coal mines. She took a job at a Pittsburgh hosiery factory when she was eleven years old. With no child labor laws or safety standards in place, Rose worked long hours alongside dangerous machinery and with little ventilation. By the time she was nineteen, she had become sick with tuberculosis, a lung disease.

Too ill to keep working in factories, Rose focused on making them safer for others. She moved to New York City, joined a workers' rights union, and became a factory inspector. In 1914, she spoke to US President Woodrow Wilson, demanding better conditions for women workers. "I am one of the thousands of women who work in the sweated trades, and have been since a child," she told the president. "Our reward is the tuberculosis sanitorium or the street."

But real change couldn't happen unless women gained suffrage, or the right to vote. Rose became a suffragist and traveled out west giving impassioned speeches that emboldened women to refuse unequal treatment. She joined National Woman's Party leader Alice Paul as a Silent Sentinel. They stood quietly in front of the White House, holding banners with messages like MR. PRESIDENT, HOW LONG MUST WOMEN WAIT FOR LIBERTY.

Rose and Alice were arrested, thrown in jail, and tortured for seven months. They went on a hunger strike to let the world know that they were political prisoners, not criminals. Rose scribbled notes on tiny pieces of paper that were snuck out of the jail to her husband and friends. "I have felt quite feeble the last few days—faint, so that I could hardly get my hair brushed," Rose wrote. "Don't let them tell you we take this well. . . . It is horrible. . . . God knows we don't want other women to have to do this over again."

The notes became famous and helped gain support for the Nineteenth Amendment, the women's voting rights law. By traveling the country, picketing the White House, and going on a hunger strike, Rose Winslow brought the world's attention to the unequal treatment of women. Her persistence led Congress to pass laws ensuring women's rights, including the right to vote.

★ Three years after the Nineteenth Amendment passed, Rose became a theatrical actress. She performed on Broadway for a few years under her birth name, Ruza Wenclawska.

★ Rose was also a poet, and her words inspired women at voting-rights rallies.

73

JOE WONG

"I'M MORE CURIOUS ABOUT PEOPLE THAN WHAT I HAD TO STUDY IN THE LAB, WHICH IS FRUIT FLIES."

The comedian Joe Wong grew up with the name Huang Xi in a small village in China. His parents expected him to work hard in school and to get a high-paying job, so he attended the Chinese Academy of Sciences. He then traveled to Houston, Texas, where he earned a PhD in biochemistry and cell biology from Rice University. Afterward he moved to Boston to do cancer research. So how did he wind up as such a popular comedian in both the United States and China?

When he was a kid, Xi enjoyed listening to a traditional kind of comedy called "crosstalk" on Chinese radio. "In crosstalk, performers play a role on stage—a tightwad, a dumb guy, or a greedy guy, etc.," he said. But there was nothing personal in crosstalk humor; the actors never spoke about their own frustrations or wacky observations. Later in life, when friends in the United States took Xi to comedy clubs, he discovered a more appealing kind of comedy: stand-up. "It's up-to-date, fast-paced, and personal," Xi said. He thought he'd be good at it.

Xi took a comedy class in Boston and performed at an open-mic night at a bar. His friends laughed . . . a little. But no one else did. They couldn't understand him. Instead of being discouraged, Xi worked on his jokes—and his English. He studied comedians like Richard Pryor and Chris Rock, who he says "taught me that comedy is a tool to deal with racism and injustice."

Xi worked as a cancer researcher by day, succeeding professionally as his parents wanted. But he also began performing at night under the stage name Joe Wong. He won first place in the Great American Comedy Festival, which led to appearances on TV shows hosted by Ellen Degeneres and David Letterman. One of his most famous moments came when he joked with good-natured Vice President Joe Biden at a dinner in Washington, DC. "I actually read your autobiography, and today I see you," Xi said to Biden. "I think the book is much better."

When Xi returned to China to perform, he discovered many changes from what it was like when he was a boy. Chinese people—especially younger ones—had become more willing to talk about themselves, a cornerstone of stand-up comedy, which Xi uses to bring about even more openness in that country. In 2013, he began hosting a hit TV show in China, and he hopes to star in a sitcom in the United States someday, too.

* When Xi was ten years old, he loved watching old Charlie Chaplin comedies with his father.

* He refers to himself as the "All-American Immigrant."

I DO MY JOB SO YOU CAN DO YOURS
NANNIES NEED
TAKE CARE of NANNIES THEY TAKE CARE of US!
DOMESTIC WORK DEMANDS RESPECT
STOP
RESPECT DOMESTIC WORKERS
TREAT US
ABUSE

BARBARA YOUNG

"IF THE WORK YOU ARE DOING IS LIFTING UP AND ENHANCING THE LIFE OF ANOTHER PERSON, THEN THAT WORK HAS VALUE."

As a bus conductor in Barbados, Barbara Young was so good at her job and at getting along with people that she became a negotiator for the country's transport board. She liked solving problems and settling arguments between workers and employers. Then the transit system cut its workforce and Barbara lost her job. With her five children fully grown, Barbara was eager to start a new life. She immigrated to New York City and found a job as a domestic worker. The term refers to workers who are employed in other people's homes as housekeepers, caregivers for older adults, or nannies who take care of children.

As a nanny, Barbara worked long hours. She had no days off and was paid much less than what she'd earned in Barbados. But Barbara needed work and she loved the baby she cared for. While taking the little girl on stroller walks to a park, Barbara became friends with other nannies. Like her, many were immigrants or refugees. All of them were women, and some were just learning to speak English. Barbara listened to their struggles and was shocked to discover that some worked even longer hours than she did with no overtime pay. Some hadn't been paid yet at all!

Studying labor rights, Barbara learned that there were no laws to protect domestic workers and no standards for payment. It was obvious to Barbara that these nannies weren't taken seriously as workers because they were women, and because they were scared of being fired or deported to their home countries if they spoke out. Barbara was afraid of losing her job, too, but she took action, and her courage ignited a new movement: the domestic workers civil rights movement. "The goal was to let people know they matter, they are important, the job they were doing was important," she said.

Barbara rallied other home workers to protest with her. They held up mops and strollers to catch the attention of lawmakers—and it worked! Barbara told the lawmakers about the problems they faced. She campaigned for six years until New York State passed the Domestic Workers' Bill of Rights in 2010. Other states soon passed similar laws, making sure domestic workers earn livable wages, overtime pay, and paid time off.

By taking action and demanding that everyone be treated fairly, Barbara ensured that millions of home care workers are respected and have laws to protect them, and that they aren't invisible anymore.

* Barbara first learned about laws for workers while taking a child-care course. She is certified in CPR (cardiopulmonary resuscitation).

* As a nanny, Barbara stuffed her purse with flyers about rights for domestic workers. She handed them out to other nannies at playgrounds, bus stops, and libraries.

AHMED ZEWAIL

"I AM AN EGYPTIAN. I AM AN ARAB. I AM AN AFRICAN. I AM MIDDLE EASTERN. I AM MEDITERRANEAN. I AM AN AMERICAN."

Ahmed Zewail grew up in a cheerful, supportive Muslim family near Alexandria, Egypt—a city he called "the home of ancient learning." Ahmed's parents dreamed that he'd study at a great university and then become a teacher. They put a sign that said DR. AHMED on his bedroom door. Ahmed did not just want to memorize facts. He said his "mind kept asking 'how' and 'why'" as he studied.

He received a scholarship to work toward his doctorate at the University of Pennsylvania in the United States in 1969. "The culture was foreign, the language was difficult, but my hopes were high," he said, recalling the experience as "the feeling of being thrown into an ocean. The ocean was full of knowledge . . . and the choice was clear: I could either learn to swim or sink."

Ahmed loved working with skilled scientists in the United States. He especially enjoyed experiments that drew on more than one form of science. When he earned his doctorate in 1974, he expected to return to Egypt and rekindle the kinds of research that had made the Islamic world the center of scientific learning centuries before. But war was raging throughout the Middle East. "Returning was important to me, but I also knew that Egypt would not be able to provide the scientific atmosphere I had enjoyed in the US," he said. An exciting opportunity brought him to the University of California, Berkeley, which he knew "was a great place for science—the BIG science." That's where he developed his new branch of research, known as femtoscience.

Chemists study chemical reactions, but most of those take place too quickly to be seen. Working with lasers that fired short pulses, Ahmed figured out how to record the shifts of chemical bonds so they could be played back as a sort of movie. The actions he recorded took place in a few femtoseconds. (A femtosecond is one millionth of a billionth of a second.) For that, he was honored with the Nobel Prize in Chemistry.

After winning the Nobel Prize, Ahmed developed the Zewail City of Science and Technology in Cairo, Egypt. It opened in 2013, linking the ancient and the modern worlds "to demonstrate the power of science in building the future."

* Ahmed wrote sixteen books and more than 600 scholarly articles. He died in 2016.

* Ahmed served as a science and technology adviser to President Barack Obama.

THE INSPIRATION BEHIND
FIRST GENERATION

It's been so meaningful for Rich and me to research and write about the incredible people in this book. There are many more trailblazers we couldn't include, and we hope that books will be written about them, too. We chose men and women who faced extraordinary obstacles yet believed in themselves, persevered, and became role models who have given back to their communities and transformed America with their genius, grit, and love.

This is the type of book I wish I'd had growing up. But because I didn't, I wrote book reports on biographies about famous men (mostly from previous centuries) who I couldn't relate to. Here in the twenty-first century, one in every six American adults (including me!) was born in another country. With so many immigrants and refugees contributing to our culture, it's important to learn about their achievements and their hardships. Newcomers have strengthened America just as much as the immigrants and refugees of past centuries, and knowing this builds unity and gives all of us the courage to become trailblazers.

Czech American Martina Navratilova, for example, could have been deported if she'd come out as gay before US immigration laws were changed in 1990. And if Barbadian American Barbara Young hadn't convinced lawmakers to pass the Domestic Workers' Bill of Rights, millions of home workers would have no employment rights. In fact, it was Barbara Young who inspired us to write this book!

Like Barbara, my grandmother Anna Koenig was a domestic worker—a live-in housekeeper—for more than thirty years. She had been a wealthy landowner, innkeeper, and chef in Yugoslavia (now Serbia), but World War II abruptly changed all of that. A concentration camp survivor, Anna arrived in Canada as a refugee, along with my mom and great-grandmother. Because she was a newcomer who spoke no English, she wasn't hired for the jobs where she was an expert. A busy family of doctors hired her to cook and clean.

I thought about my grandmother as I waited nervously to take my US citizenship test in 2016. Because of her bravery, I'd had more freedom in my life than she did, but as a new immigrant, I still felt vulnerable. I couldn't vote, and I was afraid I might be penalized for protesting injustices. But then I passed the test. And I value the freedoms and responsibilities that came with my new citizenship more than anything.

Newcomers still face prejudice in America, but Rich and I hope this book—and more importantly, *you*—will help change that! As we've seen from these thirty-six changemakers, diversity and difference aren't things to be afraid of; they're what make America great.

—Sandra Neil Wallace

★ ILLUSTRATOR'S NOTE ★

The most interesting part of my work as an illustrator is research; I specialize in portraits and I love to learn about my subjects. When I first took this project on, I had heard of about only half the people included in it. After reading about their lives and accomplishments, it was inspiring to create a piece of artwork showing each person against a background or in a pose that represents something important about them. There was a lot of sketching and going back and forth with different ideas; I spent so much time looking at my subjects' faces, it almost felt as if I became friends with some of them. (Fun fact: Soon after finishing the portrait of chef Marcus Samuelsson, I bumped into him on the street in Greenpoint, Brooklyn, where I currently live.) I'm grateful for the privilege of portraying legendary artists and thinkers, scientists, athletes, and politicians, and introducing many of them to young readers for the first time.

Working on this book was not only a great experience but also a personal one for me, as I recently moved to America from Warsaw, Poland. At the time, my then nine-year-old daughter shared her observation that the United States is not merely a country. It's a place where people from everywhere in the world come to live. Diversity is the best thing about the United States, and its greatest strength— something we ought to cherish and cultivate. Wherever my family and I end up living next, I'll always be grateful for the chance to have lived here and to have witnessed the beautiful people who come from all cultures and religions and corners of our planet, coexisting together.

– Agata Nowicka

★ ACKNOWLEDGMENTS ★

We'd like to thank our fearless editor, Deirdre Jones, for being as excited about this book as we are; book designer Karina Granda; the dedicated publishing team at Little, Brown Books for Young Readers; and Agata Nowicka for her amazing artwork. Lastly, a huge word of thanks to our literary agent, Liza Voges, for encouraging us to be trailblazers and championing our work.

– SNW and RW

BE A TRAILBLAZER!

★ Show support for new kids in school and in your neighborhood. Say hello. Show them the playground or the library. Or just smile.

★ Share foods from your culture and encourage your friends and classmates to do the same. Food is a great way to bring people together.

★ Write a letter to a refugee. Care.org has a "Letters of Hope" program that connects people with refugee children throughout the world.

★ Ask relatives about your history. When did your family first arrive in the United States? Where did they live? Where did they work? Did they face any hardships, and how did they overcome them? If your family is Native American, how has the arrival of others affected you?

★ Stand up for kids who are being bullied, and don't be afraid to tell an adult. Bullies usually stop when they realize that their victims have allies.

★ Volunteer with a local organization that supports immigrants and refugees.

★ Celebrate Immigrant Heritage Month in June and World Refugee Day on June 20.

★ Be kind to <u>EVERYONE</u>!

★ FOR MORE INFORMATION ★

To find out more about immigrants and refugees, we recommend these resources:

BOOKS

Angel Island: Gateway to Gold Mountain by Russell Freedman (Houghton Mifflin Harcourt, 2016)

Children of War: Voices of Iraqi Refugees by Deborah Ellis (Groundwood Books, 2010)

Kids Like Me: Voices of the Immigrant Experience by Judith M. Blohm and Terri Lapinsky (Nicholas Brealey, 2006)

Remix: Conversations with Immigrant Teenagers by Marina Budhos (Wipf & Stock, 2007)

Stormy Seas: Stories of Young Boat Refugees by Mary Beth Leatherdale (Annick Press, 2017)

This Land Is Our Land: A History of American Immigration by Linda Barrett Osborne (Abrams, 2016)

We Are America: A Tribute from the Heart by Walter Dean Myers (HarperCollins, 2015)

WEBSITES

American Civil Liberties Union, ACLU.org

Amnesty International, Amnesty.org

Ellis Island National Museum of Immigration, libertyellisfoundation.org/immigration-museum

I Am An Immigrant, iamanimmigrant.com

Immigration Stories of Yesterday and Today, Teacher.Scholastic.com/activities/immigration

The New Americans, PBS.org/independentlens/newamericans/

The UN Refugee Agency, UNHCR.org

Teaching Tolerance (Southern Poverty Law Center), Tolerance.org

US Committee for Refugees and Immigrants, Refugees.org

SELECTED BIBLIOGRAPHY

In researching the heroic immigrants and refugees in this book, we consulted hundreds of sources including interviews, articles from newspapers and magazines, books, documentary films, and other materials. Below is a partial list. If you'd like to learn more about the people in *First Generation*, please visit SandraNeilWallace.com and RichWallaceBooks.com for a longer list of sources.

ADEN, HALIMA

Cunningham, Erin. **"Halima Aden: 'It's Powerful to Know You Can Dress Modestly & Be Beautiful.'"** Refinery29. June 12, 2017. http://www.refinery29.com/halima-aden-hijabi-muslim-model-photos.

Shapiro, Rebecca. **"Halima Aden Becomes First Miss Minnesota Contestant to Compete in Hijab and Burkini."** *Huffington Post.* December 20, 2016. http://www.huffingtonpost.com /entry/halima-aden-becomes-first-miss-minnesota-contestant-to-compete-in-hijab-and-burkini _us_583bc177e4b09b6056010691.

Young, Molly. **"Muslim Model Halima Aden on Defying Beauty Standards."** *Allure.* June 20, 2017. https://www.allure.com/story/halima-aden-cover-story-july-2017.

ALBRIGHT, MADELEINE

Blackman, Ann. *Seasons of Her Life: A Biography of Madeleine Korbel Albright.* New York: Scribner, 1998

Curtis, Colleen. **"What the Medal of Freedom Means to Me: Madeleine Albright."** White House blog. May 30, 2012. https://obamawhitehouse.archives.gov/blog/2012/05/30/what-medal-freedom-means-me -madeleine-albright.

Drozdova, Katya, and Ruth Ediger. **"Of Putin and Pins: A Conversation with Madeleine Albright."** *Response.* July 21, 2014. http://spu.edu/depts/uc/response/new/web-features/2014/madeleine-albright.asp.

AL-HADID, DIANA

La Force, Thessaly. **"Artist Diana Al-Hadid on Fate, Form, and Freud—and Her New Exhibition at the Secession in Vienna."** *Vogue.* September 10, 2014. https://www.vogue.com/article/artist-diana-al-hadid -exhibition-vienna-secession.

Leech, Nick. **"Acclaimed Sculptor Diana Al-Hadid on Her New Show Opening at NYUAD Art Gallery."** *The National.* March 3, 2016. https://www.thenational.ae/arts-culture/acclaimed-sculptor-diana -al-hadid-on-her-new-show-opening-at-nyuad-art-gallery-1.150757.

Newell-Hanson, Alice. **"Artist Diana Al-Hadid Is Challenging Assumptions about Arabic Women."** i-D. April 13, 2015. https://i-d.vice.com/en_us/article/bjz7va/artist-diana-al-hadid-is-challenging-assumptions -about-arabic-women.

BRIN, SERGEY

Auletta, Ken. **"Searching for Trouble."** *New Yorker*, October 12, 2009.

Malseed, Mark. **"The Story of Sergey Brin."** *Moment*. May 6, 2007. http://www.momentmag.com/the -story-of-sergey-brin/.

Weinberger, Matt. **"'Outraged by This Order'—Here's the Speech Google Cofounder Sergey Brin Just Gave Attacking Trump's Immigration Ban."** *Business Insider*. January 30, 2017. http://www .businessinsider.com/google-sergey-brin-speech-trump-immigration-ban-2017-1.

CONTRERAS-SWEET, MARIA

Eilperin, Juliet. **"Obama Picks Maria Contreras-Sweet to Head SBA."** *Washington Post*, January 14, 2014. https://www.washingtonpost.com/politics/obama-picks-maria-contreras-sweet-to-head -sba/2014/01/14/8176d5c4-7d56-11e3-9556-4a4bf7bcbd84_story.html?utm_term=.107f43bdab03.

"I Am American Business: Maria Contreras-Sweet," CNBC. June 24, 2012, https://www.cnbc.com /id/100000508.

Romano-Barrera, Gloria. **"Maria Contreras-Sweet: An Inspiring New Leader at the SBA."** *Latina Style*. Accessed June 20, 2017. http://latinastyle.com/magazine/maria-contreras-sweet-an-inspiring-new-leader -at-the-sba/.

CRUZ, CELIA

"Azucar: The Life and Music of Celia Cruz." Smithsonian National Museum of American History website. Accessed June 4, 2017. http://amhistory.si.edu/celiacruz/.

Cruz, Celia, with Anna Cristina Reymundo. *Celia: My Life, an Autobiography.* New York: HarperCollins, 2005.

Pareles, Jon. **"Review/Pop; The Queen of Latin Music Takes It from the Top."** *New York Times*, December 14, 1992.

DE KOONING, WILLEM

Schjeldahl, Peter. **"Shifting Picture: A de Kooning Retrospective."** *New Yorker*, September 26, 2011.

Stevens, Mark, and Annalyn Swan. *de Kooning: An American Master.* New York: Alfred A. Knopf, 2004.

Strickland, Carol. **"Willem de Kooning: Pioneer of Abstract Art."** *Christian Science Monitor*, March 24, 1997.

DHAM, VINOD

Bach, John. **"The Technology Trailblazer."** *UC Magazine*, October 2000.

Saga, Ben. **"Vinod Dham (Biography)—Father of Pentium Chip."** Business Saga. March 16, 2016. http://businesssaga.com/vinod-dham/.

Takahashi, Dean. **"Interview with Vinod Dham, Father of the Pentium, on a life in technology and venture investing."** *Venture Beat.* July 3, 2008. https://venturebeat.com/2008/07/03/interview-with -vinod-dham-father-of-the-pentium-on-a-life-in-technology-and-venture-investing/.

DIAZ MEYER, CHERYL

Creger, Mike. **"Duluth's Own Pulitzer Prize-Winning War Photographer to Speak at Fundraiser for Relief Organization."** *Duluth News Tribune*, October 3, 2015.

"Pulitzer Prize Winner—Cheryl Diaz Meyer—the Reply," HelloPhoto. October 14, 2009. http://www. hellophoto.co.nz/showthread.php?1197-Pulitzer-Prize-winner-Cheryl-Diaz-Meyer-The-reply.

Temple, John. **"Pulitzers Lost, What a Cost,"** *Temple Talk* (blog). September 9, 2009. http://www .johntemple.net/2009/09/pulitzers-lost-what-cost-cheryl-diaz.html.

EINSTEIN, ALBERT

"Albert Einstein's Legacy as a Refugee." International Rescue Committee. July 24, 2017. https://www .rescue.org/article/albert-einsteins-legacy-refugee.

Isaacson, Walter. ***Einstein: His Life and Universe.*** New York: Simon & Schuster, 2007.

Rowe, David E. and Robert Schulmann, eds. ***Einstein on Politics***. Princeton University Press, 2007.

GIBRAN, KAHLIL

Acocella, Joan. **"Prophet Motive: The Kahlil Gibran Phenomenon."** *New Yorker*, January 7, 2008.

"Kahlil Gibran (1883-1931)," All Poetry. Accessed October 15, 2017. https://allpoetry.com/khalil-gibran.

"Kahlil Gibran: 1883–1931," Poetry Foundation. Accessed April 9, 2017. https://www.poetryfoundation .org/poets/kahlil-gibran.

GROJSMAN, SOPHIA

Berger, Paul. **"Perfume 'Nose' Conjures up Perfect Scents."** *Forward.* October 26, 2011. http://forward .com/news/144873/perfume-nose-conjures-up-perfect-scents/.

Nemy, Enid. **"In the World of Fragrance, Reputations Rest on the Nose…"** *New York Times*, February 11, 1993.

Frolova, Victoria. **"Sophia Grojsman: Perfumer Interview."** *Bois de Jasmin* (blog). March 12, 2006. https://boisdejasmin.com/2006/03/sophia_grojsman.html.

HIRONO, MAZIE

Boylan, Dan. **"The Immigrant Congresswoman."** *Midweek*, March 21, 2007. http://archives.midweek.com/content/story/midweek_coverstory/the_immigrant_congresswoman/P0/.

Dayton, Kevin. **"Mazie Hirono: From Poverty to Quiet Power."** *Honolulu Advertiser*, September 4, 2002.

LaFrance, Adrienne. **"What It's Like to Be the Only Asian-American Woman in the U.S. Senate."** Medium. January 12, 2014. https://medium.com/@adriennelaf/what-its-like-to-be-the-only-asian-american-woman-in-the-u-s-senate-6d7a07e2804e.

HUSSEIN, FATIMAH

Hirsi, Ibrahim. **"How an Athletic Program for Minneapolis Girls Led to Startup Designing Sportswear for Muslim Women Everywhere."** MinnPost. November 2, 2016. https://www.minnpost.com/new-americans/2016/11/how-athletic-program-minneapolis-girls-led-startup-designing-sportswear-muslim.

Martin, Claire. **"Putting Faith and Sports on the Same Team."** *New York Times*, January 6, 2017.

St. Anthony, Neal. **"Apparel Firm Asiya Eyes Female Sportswear Niche."** *Star Tribune*, November 6, 2016.

JAN, RAZIA

Ferringer, Megan. **"A Dangerous Idea Offers Hope for Girls in Afghanistan."** *The Rotarian*, March 19, 2014.

Khan, Adnan. **"Afghan Women's Activist Razia Jan Points the Way for Girls."** *The National*, UAE Edition. March 10, 2012. https://www.thenational.ae/lifestyle/afghan-women-s-activist-razia-jan-points-the-way-for-girls-1.361423.

Murphy, Beth. **"A First: Building a College for Rural Afghan Women."** *Islamic Monthly*. August 5, 2015. https://www.theislamicmonthly.com/a-first-building-a-college-for-rural-afghan-women/.

JONES, MOTHER

Gorn, Elliott J. *Mother Jones: The Most Dangerous Woman in America.* New York: Hill and Wang, 2001.

Kraft, Betsy Harvey. *Mother Jones: One Woman's Fight for Labor.* New York: Clarion Books, 1995.

"Mother Jones." AFL-CIO. Accessed May 5, 2017. https://aflcio.org/about/history/labor-history-people/mother-jones.

KEFLEZIGHI, MEB

Cowan, Lee. **"Meb Keflezighi: The Long Run."** CBS News. August 21, 2016. Video, 6:48. https://www
.cbsnews.com/news/meb-keflezighi-the-long-run/.

Powers, John. **"American Meb Keflezighi Wins Boston Marathon."** *Boston Globe*, April 21, 2014.

Whiteside, Kelly. **"Meb Keflezighi Carries Victims in His Heart During Boston Marathon Win."** *USA
Today*, April 21, 2014.

MA, YO-YO

Covington, Richard. **"Yo-Yo Ma's Other Passion."** *Smithsonian*, June 2002.

Jeffries, Stuart. **"Yo-Yo Ma: Bach, Big Bird and Me."** *Guardian*, July 28, 2015.

Slate, Libby. **"Yo-Yo Ma and His Passion for Musical Communication."** *Los Angeles Times*, October 26,
1988.

MIRZAKHANI, MARYAM

Carey, Bjorn. **"Stanford's Maryam Mirzakhani Wins Fields Medal."** *Stanford News*. August 12, 2014.
http://news.stanford.edu/news/2014/august/fields-medal-mirzakhani-081214.html.

Iranwire. **"Iranian Math Genius Mirzakhani Unveiled by President Rouhani."** Daily Beast. August 18,
2014. https://www.thedailybeast.com/iranian-math-genius-mirzakhani-unveiled-by-president-rouhani.

Sample, Ian. **"Fields Medal Mathematics Prize Won by Woman for First Time in Its History."** *Guardian*,
August 12, 2014.

MUIR, JOHN

Eskin, Eden Force. *John Muir.* Englewood Cliffs, NJ: Gallin House Press, 1990.

Heacox, Kim. *John Muir and the Ice That Started a Fire: How a Visionary and the Glaciers of Alaska
Changed America.* Guilford, CT: Lyons Press, 2014.

Muir, John. *Our National Parks.* Boston: Houghton, Mifflin and Co., 1901.

MUTOMBO, DIKEMBE

Bruton, F. Brinley. **"Dikembe Mutombo Proves Changing the World Isn't 'Crazy' After All."** NBC
News. December 25, 2016. https://www.nbcnews.com/news/world/dikembe-mutombo-proves-changing
-world-isn-t-crazy-after-all-n697661.

Jones, Maya A. **"Dikembe Mutombo Receives Humanitarian Award from Harvard Medical School."**
The Undefeated. May 3, 2017. https://theundefeated.com/features/dikembe-mutombo-humanitarian
-award-harvard-medical-school/.

Lee, Michael. **"Dikembe Mutombo: A Hall of Fame Player with Global Reach."** *Washington Post*, September 10, 2015.

NAVRATILOVA, MARTINA

Macur, Juliet. **"Long Before Kaepernick, There Was Navratilova."** *New York Times*, October 16, 2016.

Navratilova, Martina. *Shape Your Self: My 6-Step Diet and Fitness Plan to Achieve the Best Shape of Your Life.* Emmaus, PA: Rodale, 2006.

Schwartz, Larry. **"Martina Was Alone on Top."** ESPN. Accessed April 19, 2017. http://www.espn.com /classic/biography/s/Navratilova_Martina.html.

NOOYI, INDRA

Nilekani, Nandan. **"Personal Side of Indra Nooyi."** *Economic Times* (India), February 7, 2007.

Seabroook, John. **"Snacks for a Fat Planet."** *New Yorker*, May 16, 2011.

Stevenson, Abigail. **"Indra Nooyi: The Secret to Pepsi's Innovation."** CNBC. March 9, 2015, https://www .cnbc.com/2015/03/09/indra-nooyi-ceos-are-not-big-shots.html.

OCAMPO, ADRIANA

Lee, Peter. **"NASA Scientist Encourages Women to Reach for the Stars."** *Waterloo Region Record*, March 8, 2013.

Myhre, Jeff. **"Immigrant of the Week: Adriana Ocampo of NASA."** xpatnation. June 20, 2016. Accessed June 24, 2017. www.xpatnation.com/immigrant-of-the-week-adriana-ocampo-of-nasa.

Simón, Yara. **"Adriana Ocampo Is One of the Sheroes Behind NASA's Mission to Jupiter."** Remezcla. July 5, 2016. http://remezcla.com/culture/adriana-ocampo-juno-jupiter-nasa/.

PARK, PAULINE

Flores, Louis. **"Documentary about Activist Pauline Park Reveals a Personal Tale That Never Strays Far from Politics."** ProgressQueens. April 2, 2017. http://www.progressqueens.com/news/2017/4/2 /documentary-about-activist-pauline-park-reveals-a-personal-tale-that-never-strays-far-from-politics.

"In Her Own Image: Transgender Activist Pauline Park." The Gully. July 2, 2002. http://www.thegully .com/essays/gaymundo/020702_transgender_p_park.html.

Kowalska, Monika. **"Interview with Pauline Park."** *The Heroines of My Life* (blog). August 30, 2015. https://theheroines.blogspot.com/2015/08/interview-with-pauline-park.html.

PEI, I. M.

"Biography." Pritzker Prize. Accessed June 8, 2017. http://www.pritzkerprize.com/1983/bio.

Davidson, Justin. "A Portrait of I. M. Pei at (Nearly) 100." *New York*, April 17, 2017.

Glancey, Jonathan. "The Pei Master." *Guardian*, February 28, 2010.

RAMOS, JORGE

Finnegan, William. "The Man Who Wouldn't Sit Down." *New Yorker*, October 5, 2015.

Grove, Lloyd. "Why TV Anchor Jorge Ramos Swam Across the Rio Grande." Daily Beast. July 22, 2014. https://www.thedailybeast.com/why-tv-anchor-jorge-ramos-swam-across-the-rio-grande.

James, Meg. "Univision's Jorge Ramos a Powerful Voice on Immigration." *Los Angeles Times*, June 3, 2013.

SAMUELSSON, MARCUS

Carman, Tim. "Marcus Samuelsson on Cooking and Controversy." *Washington Post*, August 10, 2012.

Pauley, Jane. "Marcus Samuelsson: Living the Dream," CBS News. November 22, 2015. Video, 4:42. https://www.cbsnews.com/news/marcus-samuelsson-living-the-dream/.

Rayner, Jay. "Marcus Samuelsson: The Restaurant King of Harlem." *Guardian*, May 15, 2016.

SANTANA, CARLOS

Colurso, Mary. "5 Questions with Carlos Santana: Guitarist Gets Philosophical Before Concert in Birmingham." AL. March 12, 2015. http://www.al.com/entertainment/index.ssf/2015/03/carlos _santana_birmingham_conce.html.

Martin, Michel. "Carlos Santana: 'I Am a Reflection of Your Light.'" *Morning Edition*, NPR. November 4, 2014. Audio, 7:49. http://www.npr.org/2014/11/04/360092359/carlos-santana-i-am-a-reflection-of-your -light.

Santana, Carlos. *The Universal Tone: Bringing My Story to Light.* New York: Little, Brown and Company, 2014.

SEIRAWAN, YASSER

Bethea, Charles. "A Chess Renaissance in the Midwest." *New Yorker*, April 28, 2016.

Matnadze, Anna. "Interview with Yasser Seirawan." Chessdom. October 28, 2011. http://www.chessdom .com/interview-with-yasser-seirawan/.

"Yasser Seirawan: 20 Questions." KingpinChess. April 4, 2015. http://www.kingpinchess.net/2015/04 /yasser-seirawan/.

TESLA, NIKOLA

Carlson, W. Bernard. *Tesla: Inventor of the Electrical Age.* Princeton University Press, 2013.

Cheney, Margaret. *Tesla: Man out of Time.* New York: Dorset Press, 1981.

Grubin, David. *Tesla: Visionary or Madman?* American Experience, aired October 18, 2016, DVD.

ULUKAYA, HAMDI

Gelles, David. **"For Helping Immigrants, Chobani's Founder Draws Threats."** *New York Times*, October 31, 2016.

Gross, Daniel. **"It's All Greek to Him: Chobani's Unlikely Success Story."** *Newsweek*, June 12, 2013.

McCandless, Brit. **"Chobani's Chief Taster."** *60 Minutes* on CBS. April 9, 2017. https://www.cbsnews.com/news/chobani-yogurt-chief-taster/.

WINSLOW, ROSE

Stevens, Doris. *Jailed for Freedom: American Women Win the Vote.* Salem, NH: Ayer Co., 1990. First published 1920 by Boni and Liveright (New York).

"Women Use Sharp Terms to Wilson." *New York Times*, February 3, 1914.

"Women We Celebrate: Rose Winslow." National Woman's Party. Accessed June 18, 2017. http://nationalwomansparty.org/womenwecelebrate/rose-winslow/.

WONG, JOE

Beam, Christopher. **"Can China Take a Joke?"** *New York Times Magazine*, May 21, 2015.

Fuchs, Chris. **"Off Color: Joe Wong Is on a Mission to Make China Laugh."** NBC News. April 20, 2015. https://www.nbcnews.com/news/asian-america/color-joe-wong-mission-make-china-laugh-n337131.

Kazer, William. **"Killing Crowds in Two Languages: Q&A with Comedian Joe Wong."** *China Real Time Report* (blog). *Wall Street Journal*, March 16, 2015. https://blogs.wsj.com/chinarealtime/2015/03/16/killing-crowds-in-two-languages-qa-with-comedian-joe-wong/.

YOUNG, BARBARA

"Barbara Young," *Encore.* Accessed April 15, 2017. https://encore.org/purpose-prize/barbara-young/.

Raab, Barbara. **"From Nanny to National Organizer: Helping Domestic Workers Stand Up for Their Rights."** NBC News. December 18, 2013. https://www.nbcnews.com/feature/in-plain-sight/nanny-national-organizer-helping-domestic-workers-stand-their-rights-f2D11767824.

Ratner, Lizzy. **"Domestic Workers in New York Getting Closer to Having Their Own Bill of Rights."** AlterNet. September 11, 2009. https://www.alternet.org/story/142586/domestic_workers_in_new_york _getting_closer_to_having_their_own_bill_of_rights.

ZEWAIL, AHMED

"Ahmed Zewail—Biographical." Nobel Prize. Accessed May 9, 2017. https://www.nobelprize.org/nobel _prizes/chemistry/laureates/1999/zewail-bio.html.

Gedik, Nuh. **"Science in the Islamic World: An Interview with Nobel Laureate Ahmed Zewail."** *Fountain*, January–February 2009.

Pipkin, Turk, dir. ***Nobelity.*** Monterey Media, 2006, DVD.

Will Wrobel

Investigative journalists **SANDRA NEIL WALLACE** and **RICH WALLACE** are award-winning novelists and nonfiction authors of books like *Blood Brother: Jonathan Daniels and His Sacrifice for Civil Rights* and *Bound by Ice: A True North Pole Survival Story*. Sandra is a former news anchor and ESPN sportscaster. The daughter of a refugee, she became a US citizen in 2016. Rich was a longtime senior editor at *Highlights for Children* magazine. Both Sandra and Rich are members of the advisory council for the Cohen Center for Holocaust and Genocide Studies at Keene State College and are founding members of the Keene Immigrant and Refugee Partnership. They live in New Hampshire.

Maria Zaleska

AGATA NOWICKA is an illustrator and a comics artist. She spent her childhood drawing on everything with everything, including her mother's red lipstick on the staircase walls. She became an illustrator because she never wanted to stop drawing. Agata immigrated to the United States from Warsaw, Poland, and now lives in New York City.